THE UNCORRUPTED
STOCK PICKER

The Uncorrupted
Stock Picker

By
Richard C. Putz
and
Richard L. Spellman, Jr.

The North River Press Publishing Corporation

Additional copies can be obtained from
your local bookstore or the publisher:

The North River Press Publishing Corporation
P.O. Box 567
Great Barrington, Massachusetts 01230
(800) 486-2665 or (413) 528-0034

www.northriverpress.com

Copyright © 2003 Richard C. Putz and Richard L. Spellman, Jr.

All rights reserved. No part of this book may be reproduced or utilized in any form or by any means, electronic or mechanical, including photocopying, recording, or any information storage and retrieval system, without permission in writing from the publisher.

Manufactured in the United States of America.

ISBN: 0-88427-174-9

Contents

INTRODUCTION	1
CHAPTER ONE The Summarized Self-Sufficient Investor	3
CHAPTER TWO The Basics of Investing	7
CHAPTER THREE How the Market Values Stock: The Roadmap Model	16
CHAPTER FOUR Taking the Voodoo Out of Company Analysis	35
CHAPTER FIVE Using the Roadmap Model	67
CHAPTER SIX Case Studies of Publicly Traded Companies	75
APPENDIX Installing and Using the TOC Pattern Software Templates	87
BIBLIOGRAPHY	93

THE UNCORRUPTED
STOCK PICKER

Introduction

The theme of this book is that the key to investment success is not just technical mastery of charts, diagrams, financial algorithms and dartboards, but also the ability to see and apply everyday management principles using a commonsense approach to discover patterns and their movement toward success and the goal or movement away from the goal.

We therefore address this book to both the average investor who is trying to build a retirement nest egg and to the professional advisors who seek new ways to help their clients understand when to invest in companies, and more importantly, why they should invest in certain companies or others even when it appears contrary to popular notions of the day. To that end we would like to thank our many friends and colleagues who listened to us and challenged us as we presented findings to them for their feedback and comments. For they are the people who are working hard every day of their life building that retirement nest egg.

We mention all this because we believe it is fundamental to the way one has to think about the world around us and especially about the companies we invest in. After all a company is nothing more than human beings working together to achieve a goal. The question becomes how well they understand each other, work together and steer the ship toward the goal, especially in rough waters. The fundamental research process is just asking the right questions, gathering the data that is public information or provided by the companies themselves, compiling the data into pattern categories, and then the hard part. Using your knowledge and wisdom to understand the data and make a rational decision. There is, in other words, no hope or belief of a definitive answer to the question: "Is this the right company to invest in that will make me rich tomorrow?" What the patterns and TOC tools do show us is that the process is one that is committed to an ongoing process of updating and revision and monitoring to watch for shifting patterns, and comparing the patterns to each other and against each other to understand the trend.

Given the kind of world we live in and the volatility of the stock market, let alone the managers of many of the companies, the single most important variable becomes your thinking processes and your ability to trust your intuition.

Something Every Investor should know....

The Roadmap tool is a powerful investment analytical tool, as you shall soon see. However, the tool is dependent on data gathered from financial reports provided by the very companies we wish to analyze. The tool is not built to identify fallacious or misleading reporting, or to identify off-balance sheet transactions. The tool is dependent on accurate and true financial reporting.

We are convinced that financial reporting is more reliable today since the accounting problems have surfaced. Much like the person who has heart bypass surgery is far healthier than before the operation, and in most cases the probability of a heart attack is much lower than before the surgery, so we are certain the field of accounting and corporate financial reporting is already in far better shape now than prior to the revelations of inappropriate business practices, because the cleanup is well underway.

CHAPTER ONE
The Summarized Self-Sufficient Investor

The premise of this book is that there is a new way of doing stock analysis for the long term. It involves a win-win mentality and is very different from what you hear from the "experts."

The way most of us have invested in the past will not and should not survive. Investing on "hot tips" is like pulling the one-armed bandit at the casino. Yes someone will win sooner or later, but 70% will always lose. You must be company-focused; focused on what makes the company a success, how it operates and wins in the marketplace. You must also be able to, and this is the hard part, roll with the punches. Patience is mandatory when investing in common stocks. If you do not have patience it would be better to put your money elsewhere.

There are two major pillars of the Self-Sufficient Investor which will be explained in this book.

1. Patterns – Patterns are champions of investing trends and initiatives
   - Patterns show the business process issues first.
   - Theory of Constraints (TOC) – This defines the nature of patterns and uses Throughput, Inventory and Operating Expenses as measurements.
   - The decision processes must be centered on pattern movement: *Is the company at this time moving towards the goal or away from the goal?*

2. Your Competencies – Competencies is addressed with regard to the tools and methods used in investing. The ability to mesh these tools and methods together is competency; your ability

to use various tools and methods to check and balance is your intuition about investing.
- You can think of competency with respect to the three basic questions of Theory of Constraints: What to Change; What to Change To; and How to make that Change Happen.
- The patterns express competency in understanding: How companies Expand Markets; Retain Customers and Improve Efficiencies.

The book makes a case for personalization of information that only a few years ago was not readily available to the retail investor. Do you remember buying the late edition of the local newspaper to get the afternoon markets, calling your broker after the close for quotes or waiting for the weekend financial newspapers to try to make sense of it all? Today there is instantaneous information on Cable TV and the Internet: the shift in "power" has moved from the retail broker to you the consumer/customer and real investor, the one who really counts.

More and more companies will focus on business models that concentrate on adding value to existing services, and the pattern models will help you identify their success or failure and know when the pattern is shifting.

Convergence in the investing world is a much bigger trend than currently understood. The basic premise of the Internet is that it enables convergence—the bringing of information to your fingertips that at one time were only in the hands of the investing wizards. If you're an investor and you're not moving up or down the value chain to provide yourself with the best information, you're doomed.

Digitization enables an investor the luxury of speed (compression), and blends products and services (informatization) together so the investor can make intelligent decisions and build relevant models.

Informatization is about making investors smart. By squeezing information, or added value out of companies or services, you can potentially build new and exciting goal pattern models.

By showing various companies in the case studies, the one idea we hope you walk away with is to create a strategy which will include various initiatives and companies in your portfolio. That way you're not betting the farm on new, unproven companies or a particular technology, and you're also not at risk of getting left behind the field. One important concept is that if your investments will move from good to bad with time, the pattern model approach should assist you in monitoring shifting patterns, collapsing patterns and recognizing emerging patterns.

So in summary, here are a few steps that are necessary to build your models:

1. Identify the companies that are candidates to get mapped in patterns, according to your know-how, experience and belief system, and most of all your pre-defined investment program.
2. Group the companies according to industry and goals to do the research.
3. Identify the financial line items in company annual or quarterly reports, or from third party providers, as to what pattern in the model they correspond to, i.e., the three major patterns: Throughput Patterns, Inventory Patterns, and Goal Patterns.
4. Run the models and analyze.
5. At the end of the prioritization and analysis you should have a strong conclusion, and know the companies you wish to invest in for the next several years.
6. Finally, you need to consider how a new investment in a company will effect your current portfolio. You also need to assess how big you want your portfolio, how much diversification, how much concentration.
7. Remember, you do not necessarily need a large portfolio—a few well researched companies that are consistent with your investment goals can offer superior returns to a larger portfolio that is poorly assembled because of shoddy research.
8. You can use these patterns and models to analyze existing companies, emerging companies and companies that are "re-inventing" themselves.

Day trading, dot coms with no earnings, options and futures speculation, investments mismatched to peoples' objectives and needs, unreliable research, fallacious accounting...

We mean no slight to the thousands of honest, dedicated professionals in the financial world—brokers, analysts and accountants. But lets face it, our trust has been shattered. Recently, Peter Lynch urged Americans to have faith in the American capitalist system. Investing, as opposed to blind speculation, is an act of faith, but an act that can be done with knowledge, intelligence and hard work. We believe the problems we face present opportunities to the investor who is willing to put in hard work. We believe the Roadmap tool and TOC thinking processes will help you become a better researcher of common stocks and, in the long term, a more successful investor.

CHAPTER TWO
The Basics of Investing

Much has been written on the art and science of investing. Great minds and disciplined souls have researched and reasoned over the markets, indeed, they have struggled and succeeded in profiting in their investments in the world of debt and equity, also known as bonds and stocks. There is a canon of remarkable work done in this field, and the writers of this book have great respect for those who have shared their work: Benjamin Graham, John Templeton, John Bogle, Warren Buffett, John Neff, Peter Lynch, Charles Ellis, to name a few. These individuals agree on some things and disagree on others, yet from each one can learn important lessons. There is a consistency about what is essential to successful investing in the work of each of these men.

In this book we focus on the development of the study of investing, and methods used to analyze a company from the perspective of economic patterns.

"Economics" is considered and viewed as the "theoretical" cousin of accounting and finance. The world of economics comprises more than finance and accounting information. It incorporates the study of human behavior as it relates to the use, consumption and utilization of money, people, ideas, inventory and goals to satisfy the needs and wants of the company, the investors and the marketplace. Economics is always focused on the "methods" of organizing the world of production, how the goods get distributed and the marketplace consumption of goods and services. We believe the key distinction between accounting and economics can be found in the word itself and its origin. Economics comes from two Greek words: *oikos*, which means "house," and the Greek word *nemein*, which means, "to manage." So economics really means how we manage the house we live in. When Dr. Eliyahu M. Goldratt created the method called ***The Theory of Constraints*** (TOC), we believe he was laying the foundation not for a study of TOC accounting but the study of TOC economics. The writings of Dr. Goldratt and many others are truly about the management of one's house---one's business house. A house well managed is a house that will withstand the test of time. The basic lessons they teach us are:

1. To be successful one must have a strategy, or program which includes goals for the overall investment program, as well as for each portion of the program. A simple example of this is that monies targeted for college 7 years out will have different goals than monies invested for retirement 30 years away. Once the goals are set, strategies must be developed to achieve those goals. Included in these strategies is the important assessment of the investor's ability to handle different degrees of risk. Managing risk is critical. The investor, who cannot sleep unless his money is safe behind bank vaults, insured by the FDIC, would have far fewer options than the investor who can live easily with his money invested in volatile markets. As the strategies are executed, rational and emotional discipline must be exercised to avoid the common error of switching tactics or investment vehicles in an attempt to offset short-term fears or unwarranted near-term optimism. Which brings us to the second lesson.

2. The successful investor invests for the long term. History tells us that overtime common stocks will return somewhere between 9%-11%, and the longer they are held, the lower the probability of losing money. Further, it is impossible to time the market. In fact, most of the large gains in the stock market happen in very few time periods, around 7% of the available trading time. When these large moves happen is anyone's guess; what is important is to be invested in the market when they happen.

3. Take advantage of the great benefits of compound returns. A long-term program yields the benefits of compounded returns. Regardless of the investment vehicle chosen, the ability to have monies earned from your investments put back to work or to continue growing your portfolio is the single greatest advantage you gain in your investment program.

4. It is extraordinarily difficult for the professional money manager to consistently outperform the market, especially in rising markets. The data has been consistent on this topic for over 15 years. With the ever increasing availability of information and competition among professional money managers, it becomes harder and harder for any one manager to outperform his peers for a prolonged period of time. Certainly it has happened. Peter Lynch is one who bucked this trend in the eighties. However, the investor's odds of picking the next Lynch, or Templeton, out of thousands of funds are slim. Investors need to consider indexing as an alternative. An index fund, which is a passively managed fund, will by definition provide better than average returns, since a large majority of alternatives will under perform the broad based indices. Another benefit is that being a passive investment there is far less trading in these funds, and therefore, lower costs. Putting a portion of your funds in an index fund provides a solid base. However, in a flat market, or a market expected to offer very modest growth, an index fund will not be very attractive. Many experts believe the current period beginning in 2000, and continuing for several years, may well be a flat market, much like the 1970s. So while indexing offers one strategy for a low cost, passively managed strategy, the possibility of a stagnant market leads to the next alternative.

5. Avoid focusing on "the Market" and instead look for undervalued opportunities. We are inundated with news on what "the market" is doing. Is the market up or down? Over awareness of the market can lead to the wrong conclusions. Templeton and Buffett made millions by looking for undervalued stocks, regardless of what direction the market took. (This does not mean buying stocks that have low share prices. The term cheap means something very different.) The key lesson: find stocks whose per share value is trading at a discount to its real or intrinsic value. This is far more difficult than it seems. It requires gathering the right reports, analyzing and interpreting the reports, and coming to the right conclusions about the prospects of a company's future. It also requires an analysis of the qualitative aspects of the company. In the 1970s it was the investors and fund managers such as John Neff who were most successful by finding great bargains in stocks.

6. Diversify intelligently. It has become a truth universally acknowledged that a broadly diversified portfolio of many stocks is a wise investment strategy. Surely diversification is necessary, but just adding a large number of positions does not guarantee better results. In fact, some believe, Buffett among them, that over diversification leads to mediocrity. Buffett believes, according to Robert Hagstrom, that a few select positions well-researched and purchased at a discount to their intrinsic value will, over the long term, provide better returns than a portfolio of hundreds of stocks across several industry groups. Further, the successful investor diversifies his portfolio across stocks, bonds, and cash (also known as asset allocation) depending on business conditions and his own needs. The successful investor also diversifies over time, staging his investments over regular intervals.

7. Keep the costs of investing as low as possible. We are not talking about the price of a stock or bond here, or the asset value of a mutual fund. We are referring to the operational costs of investing. Such expenses as commissions, advisory fees, mutual fund expense ratios and so forth are a very important factor in determining the net results of your investment program. Wrap fees of 1%-3% may not sound like much. However when charged against your total assets, compounded year after year, the erosion of your net gains is substantial, if not downright frightening. The investor must consider these operational costs when deciding on which vehicles he will invest in.

8. Taxes, taxes, taxes. The investor needs to take advantage of the array of qualified plans available to him: 401-K's, IRA's, estate planning and so forth to minimize the effect of taxes. In addition, he needs to take into consideration the tax consequences of the strategies he chooses in his non tax-qualified accounts. Short-term trading produces many short-term capital gains that have to be realized as ordinary income. Dividends produce the same problem. Many investors search out companies that have a consistent record of increasing dividend payouts. They view such increases as a sign of a company's financial health and growth prospects, which is indeed true. However, Warren Buffett years ago figured out that it was far better for a company that he felt was an attractive investment option to reinvest its profits, increase growth, and avoid a taxable event for the shareholder. Tax deferred compound growth in a non-tax-qualified investment!

9. A successful investor does his homework. The successful investor avoids hot tips, word of mouth can't miss opportunities, the latest fad, and the monthly magazine top 10 mutual fund lists. (If these funds are so good, why are they going to have a new list next month?). In his highly entertaining *One Up on Wall Street*, Peter Lynch argues that the average investor is much closer to the companies that the institutional analyst and money managers spend so much time pulling apart on paper and in investor relation meetings. With a little homework, Lynch says, the average person can get a jump on the professionals and earn superior returns. We agree with Lynch's conclusions concerning the potential for the average investor, and this book is an answer to those confused people who want a better way to do the homework, at least the quantitative homework.

Summing the nine lessons. This very brief introduction offers some broad concepts that may appear contradictory at first but taken as a whole are really quite complimentary. The implications are clear. Build a foundation of conservatively managed assets, beginning with tax-advantaged retirement and education savings plans. Contribute regularly, take advantage of long term compounding, and invest in low cost passively managed index funds. With a significant portion of your assets invested in this manner, you have gone a long way towards diversifying away your market risk. With the remainder of your funds, usually those in non tax-qualified plans, you can seek out undervalued opportunities in the stock and bond markets in select targeted securities.

We felt it would very irresponsible to put out yet another book on stock picking, without an appropriate context as described above. Our methods promise no instant riches, undiscovered treasure chests, or lost fortunes. If you are seeking instant wealth, and are willing to accept the reality that you will, in all likelihood, lose your money, go seek counsel from the day trading or option strategy books. If you do not have that much time, buy a lottery ticket. We believe that the successful investor is a "plodder," a person with achievable goals, and a patient strategy to accomplish those goals. This book, in our minds, follows this great tradition of investing logic. What we present here is a model that enhances one's ability to do fundamental financial analysis, and presents an alternative view to traditional financial methods. The model will shed a more accurate picture of the current strength and future prospects for a given company, and help determine a stock price range where one could buy shares at a discount to the true intrinsic value of that company. Without defining an investment program as outlined above, use of this model may provide some haphazard gains, however it is very likely that the results will be mixed because the lack of formal discipline will cause many mistakes in judgment. On the other hand, if the investor is willing to be disciplined in his overall program, we are confident that this model will significantly enhance your portfolio's returns.

Finding the Information Few people would argue that in order to invest wisely a person needs to be informed. However, it requires a great deal of time and effort to gather the appropriate data, crunch the numbers and arrive at the correct conclusions. And that is just the quantitative side. Peter Lynch describes visits to corporate headquarters and other qualitative assessment activities as critical to a thorough evaluation of a company prior to investing in its stock. Indeed, one should approach an investment in the common stock of a corporation no differently than if you were asked to invest in your brother-in-laws laundry business. You are putting capital into a business because you believe, after kicking all the tires, that this investment offers a reasonable expectation of returning your money with a tidy profit, with an acceptable degree of risk. Further, this company also offers probabilities of returns that exceed the other available alternatives (other companies, other investment vehicles) or at least offer some other material advantage such as diversification, asset allocation or philanthropy.

For most of us with day jobs, families, and other life interests, such thorough research is difficult at best and impossible quite often. We can hardly imagine people dusting off their college finance textbooks as they try to remember the formulas for various financial ratios, sifting through a slew of financial reports, pro forma earnings statements and so on (all the while wondering if the reports are fully and truthfully disclosing the activities of the company). That is if they know what reports to acquire and where to get them. Then, after identifying a company with great looking numbers, running out to find out all they can about who runs the place, and what they are all about. It is rare, I am sure, that the average guy can get an appointment to interview the CEO of a Fortune 1000 company because he wants to buy 100 shares.

The huge popularity of mutual fund investing is a very rational response to this dilemma, and for many people, the best response. Should this be your situation entirely, stop here, and go read Bogle on Mutual Funds. For those who still want to pursue common stock investing, there is no way around the dilemma. No, you are not going to get a tour of the corporate headquarters, or a seat at the institutional investor relations meetings. But there is enough information available if you are willing to seek it out.

Financial reports. The Internet has become the best friend of the financial data gatherer. Almost every company has, on its website, a section entitled Investor Relations. On some sites, it may be hidden under the About Us, or How to Contact Us, sections. On these pages you should find the last couple of Annual Reports. They can be a pain to download because they contain lots of graphics (a notable exception being Berkshire Hathaway, Warren Buffett's company). Often, the site makes provisions for downloading just the financials, which helps reduce downloading time and saves disk space. You will also need the Quarterly Reports, or 10-Q's. Some companies also keep these on their web sites, but many do not. However there is a wonderful site provided by the U.S. Securities and Exchange Commission (SEC), the EDGAR Archives (http://www.sec.gov/cgi-bin/srch-edgar). This site maintains all the required financial reports of corporations since 1993. Although the search engine is a bit awkward, with a little perseverance you will find the 10-Q's and other documents should you require them. There are several other search engines that specialize in annual reports, should you have trouble with EDGAR.

Services such as Value Line, Standard and Poor's or Moody's are high quality organizations that can also be helpful, but in our view, to utilize this model, they are unnecessary. They are usually kept in public libraries. However, the information can be unreliable because it may not be current or is not well maintained. Of course they are online, and you will need to subscribe if you wish to use their services.

Qualitative vs. quantitative analysis. The model presented in this book will drive your quantitative analysis, and will also set the stage for your qualitative assessment of the operations of the company. Because the model is based on the Theory of Constraints, it will help drive your evaluations of the company. The various factors that TOC emphasizes will point to strengths or weaknesses in the strategy, tactics and operations of the company, and will help provide a forward-looking assessment of the company's future prospects. Nevertheless, further work needs to be done beyond the financial reports. A thoroughly researched assessment of a company includes evaluations of the quality of management, marketing strategy, corporate policy and so forth. For most of us, we will need to rely on business periodicals: The Wall Street Journal, Forbes, Fortune, Business Week and the like.

There are two other analysis tools in the marketplace that you may come across and you should have some familiarity with them: Economic Value Added, better known as EVA®, and Market Value Added, better known as MVA®. EVA was created by the consulting firm called Stern Stewart & Associates.

The premise is based on cash flow that is discounted and the basic formula for EVA is: EVA = Net Operating Profits after tax – book value x cost of capital. In the world of MVA the basic formula is: MVA = cash IN (investor and lender contributions) – Cash OUT (What they as investors or bankers could sell their interests for today). The reason we point this out is that in the world of TOC there are many who believe that EVA and MVA can be tools used as a TOC indicator. We are not going to enter into the debate of whether they could be used or not. But merely want to point out some of the contemporary thought that is circulating in the world of TOC.

A great financial report may be clouded by recent changes in personnel or direction or market conditions that could make a company unattractive. Sometimes your qualitative evaluations will lead you to decide that there are too many uncertain or negative factors (a new CEO, regulatory changes, a new competitive product). Although, it is disappointing when the model points you to a company that your qualitative assessment finds problems with, the good news is you avoided a potential high-risk investment. Further, such companies can be kept on a watch list to see if their prospects improve. Other times, the combined qualitative/quantitative research will lead us to where we really want to play: undervalued companies! The model can help identify companies whose stock is truly trading at a discount to its intrinsic value, and the quantitative factors can help confirm the model's conclusions. The company has a new EVP of marketing, or a new product, or has recently streamlined its operations. These kinds of activities will normally be present when the financials, after being run through the model, identify an undervalued company.

Conclusion. No one system, or analytical tool, can provide a foolproof approach to successful investing. The market is too broad, complex and diverse. What this book offers is a different method or way of thinking about what is important when evaluating the future prospects of a company. Theory of Constraints thinking offers a different perspective on what to measure of a company's activities, and how to capture those metrics in a broad sense. The investment analysis model provided here is designed to be an aid in an overall thought process in stock selection.

We have found the model to provide important insights into the strength or weakness of a company, as well as guidance as to when a company is over or under valued. Used in tandem with a solid qualitative analysis of the company in question, and the macro-environment as a whole (economic and political environment), we are confident the reader will enjoy greater success in his search for higher returns and lower risk.

CHAPTER THREE
How the Market Values Stock: The Roadmap Model

To understand how the market values stocks we must consider the following questions.

- Do prices in economic markets really reflect TOC Patterns?

- Unlike bonds, stocks do not have contractually specified cash flows and a date when principal is repaid. Bonds therefore have recognizable patterns. We have to ask: Exactly what patterns do stock prices actually reflect?

- How do the TOC Pattern Value Drivers—namely, Throughput, Operating Expenses, and Inventory—affect pattern recognition?

- How do the Other Value Determinants affect shareholder pattern?

- How do the pattern drivers and determinants fit together to create the Pattern Value Roadmap?

- What is the value of the company today? What will it be worth in two, three or even five years?

- Are the patterns that are reflective of the company shifting negatively? Or becoming obsolete?

- What patterns will capture growth or show determination against the growth?

- Does this company have a pattern of thinking Customer Back and not Company Forward? (Recognizing customer patterns and change).

- Are the movements in the patterns towards the goal of the company? Is the company increasing profits, increasing cash flow, having satisfied customers and committed and empowered employees?

- Is the company's management team "thinking" in terms of How to Expand Markets, Retain Customers and Improve Efficiencies?

Our ability to answer these questions rests on our understanding of

Six essential ideas:

1. You can visualize the movement of the pattern of a stock—its pattern value—by analyzing free cash flows and relating them back to the patterns in TOC.

2. The market value of a company should be reflective of the power of the patterns that are recognized and understood in the company in creating and capturing value and profits.

3. A core pattern exists in three states of measurements: Throughput, Inventory and Operating Expenses. Subsequent patterns develop based on these three.

4. Pattern movement from Revenue to Profit and Cash flow.

5. Pattern movement from Company power to Customer power.

6. Pattern movements from technology and processes to business design and innovation. What patterns must a manager recognize in the business in order to make a profit? Is there a pattern more dominant than others?

Synergy in the Investing Roadmap Model

In this chapter we will discuss the "roadmap" to understanding patterns based on Theory of Constraints and "Economic Root Cause Analysis" along with traditional economic analysis, traditional public reporting and various management accounting principles and values that interplay. In the traditional models you forecast cash flows to estimate a stock's value. In Theory of Constraints we reverse the process. This process begins with a combination of sources of information—to determine the pattern expectations that justify the price you should feel comfortable paying for a stock. Those outlooks and patterns, in turn, serve as the benchmark for buy, sell, or hold decisions. The "roadmap" is intended to be supplementary to, and is not a replacement for, traditional economic accounting that measures value realized through transactions with third parties. As a matter of fact, the patterns that we believe demonstrate the principles of TOC, the patterns of Throughput, Inventory and Operating Expense all contain base line items found in traditional management accounting and GAAP reporting and on the companies web sites.

Most previous attempts to measure value have focused only on shareholder value. We believe that examining TOC patterns has a broader focus, and measures economic value created for all key stakeholders: Shareholders, Partners, Suppliers, Customers, Management and Employees. It is increasingly important for enterprises to measure value created for customers, employees, and shareholders to make sure the company is viable today and in the future. Keep in mind that when looking at a company you are asking yourself "does this company focus on expanding its markets, retaining its customers and improving its efficiencies."

In shifting the focus from shareholders to stakeholders, one of the challenges that needs to be addressed is obtaining the information needed to understand the pattern in TOC value creation from all the stakeholder perspectives. In the TOC value creation patterns, stakeholders of the enterprise are not simply passive recipients of information, but have the opportunity to understand movement in key patterns that will effect the company as an ongoing concern. As an investor you should be looking for this movement and understanding in the company. The model presupposes you have done your homework and understand the management philosophy of the company.

Patterns: What are they?

Let us begin with what we mean by Patterns. Dr. Donn Novotny, Ph.D., a well-known authority on the Theory of Constraints and working colleague of Dr. Goldratt, uses a medical metaphor to explain patterns. He often explains to his clients and students that a doctor uses pattern recognition as a diagnostic tool. The doctor will ask a series of probing questions along with sensory input, such as visual and touch, to gather data. The doctor then begins a process of connecting the discovered symptoms and links them to causes. With that insight the doctor is able to develop a powerful analysis of why the person is sick and thus be able to prescribe the necessary treatment to bring the patient to health.

This process is the same for businesses, organizations and for investing. The intelligent investor is astute at understanding patterns in companies that will have an effect on the market value that company commands. Companies are shaped and re-shaped by patterns that surround them in the marketplace. The ability to know patterns, understand patterns and anticipate how the world will change when patterns develop, shift, move or fade is key for the intelligent investor. Like the doctor, connecting symptoms to causes creates a diagnosis and in turn a treatment plan. In business we call this a strategy, and this strategy should lead to the goal of profitability. This is what pattern understanding is all about.

Keep in mind, that when change in the market place is occurring rapidly, when the world seems to be in chaos, and disruption is the theme of the week, pattern recognition and understanding is critical. For it is during these market conditions that the best and worst of investment decisions are made.

Just knowing patterns will not give you a guarantee of successful investing. In chapter four we will discuss trends and questions you need to know and understand to gain insights into the patterns and their movement. As in all investing, the skill is in the knowledge and wisdom of the individual doing the investing.

Patterns are reflections of the strategy of the business. Since investors are basically outsiders we are not privy to the day-to-day decision making acts of the management team at a company. This book shows how to look at patterns reflective of the principles of the Theory of Constraints and thus on what makes a company move towards the goal of profitability. We have attempted to align various nuggets of data from financial reports that are reflective of movement in patterns. The financial data can be thought of as the symptoms or effects. Understanding how the pattern is constructed helps us understand the causes.

Capital markets are missing important information investors need.

People who work day by day in the world of capital markets are not routinely thinking in terms of TOC Patterns. Capital markets are driven by valuation and what comprises that valuation. The focus is on the line items that drive stock price. TOC patterns and TOC Thinking Processes are holistic by design. In the world of TOC a company is viewed as a holistic enterprise. The view is to have everyone in the company focus on the goal of the company, not on their individual silos. Once again think in terms of a chain with a series of links. A chain is only as strong as the weakest link. Think in terms of the greater good of the chain, not the individual link. We believe that with an understanding of the basic tenants of TOC and the related patterns, investors will be better able to monitor shifts in those patterns whether they are positive or negative, and thus gain knowledge about the patterns and the company and be able to make a decision as to the viability of the patterns, the company and the investment as a whole.

Management guru and thought leader Peter Drucker has criticized accounting for being too inward looking (focusing exclusively on an enterprise's internal processes and costs) whereas developing *holistic information*, he explains, is going to be the next information frontier. We believe that the models found in TOC will enable stakeholders to view their enterprises with a more holistic understanding.

Strategy thought-leader, author and executive coach to many of the global 2000 companies, Henry Mintzberg, has argued that enterprise managers need powerful but *comprehensible models* to help them make appropriate choices. But Mintzberg states that traditional accounting statements do not, in the case of knowledge/pattern intensive companies, provide models or patterns relating future returns to past and present activities. It is not that traditional management accounting, which has been fine tuned, tweaked, baked, fluffed, buffed and urbanized since the Middle Ages, does not have an important and continuing role to play in understanding the value of a company. The problem is that it does not handle the emerging requirements of the leading innovative companies, knowledge of intense companies and intellectual capital intense companies that are surviving in the new world of e-commerce, globalization, networking, and deep knowledge concentration. Companies are moving towards a world of real time enterprises and zero latency with regard to information. This is extremely important and relevant to companies that focus on expanding markets and retaining customers. As this operational pattern continues to evolve, new stock market values will arise in companies capable of addressing the real time enterprise. Therefore the important continuing role traditional accounting plays needs to be fully understood by all stakeholders. We need both the time-tested rigor of traditional accounting in seeking objective, transaction-based evidence of value realization—and some new parallel approach of tracking value creation in recognizing patterns and pattern movements.

We believe that the use of traditional reporting found in management accounting and SEC reports, and taking various line items that are relative to pattern movement and re-grouping them into what we call TOC patterns will aid investors in analyzing companies as to the potential success and growth of the company.

Synergy in the Patterns

Investing is a process of employing several different tools and activities involving the analysis of the economic condition of specific companies, groups of companies, industries, enterprises and supply chains, or the business climate as a whole, in order to minimize or eliminate certain risks in making decisions on which companies to invest in. At a macro level, what the investor is seeking to conclude are two basic facts: first, what is the economic value of a company today based on the pattern recognition of the past, and what it's future economic value will be, and second, based on that value, what is an acceptable price to pay for the shares of that company's stock.

What is an investor using TOC tools and methods really trying to understand about a company? The answer is: cash flow and the good leverage of business assets towards achieving the goal of the company. You are trying to understand if this company is focused on improving the roadmap of continuous improvement in expanding its markets, retaining its customers and improving the overall efficiency of the company.

TOC tools and methods are truly applicable to any process in any organization. This includes companies that are classified as distribution, retail, financial institutions, universities, hospitals, service providers of all varieties, government and, of course, manufacturing where the tools and methods were first used with great success. The KEY point to realize about the TOC Thinking Processes is understanding how the tools are designed to be used for analyzing investment opportunities, venture opportunities and mergers & acquisition opportunities in a cross section of industry sectors and businesses, not just how the tools are used to understand internal operations within a company.

The central theme in the Theory of Constraints is that every real system, such as a publicly traded enterprise, must have at least one, if not several constraints. If it were not true, then the enterprise would produce an infinite amount of whatever it strives for in the market. If it helps to think of constraints as roadblocks, bottlenecks or clogs in the operation, then feel free to substitute the nomenclature.

Because a constraint is a factor that limits the company from getting more of whatever it strives for, then the board of directors and the business management team who are measured by the flow of profits must manage the constraint(s). There really is no choice in the matter. Management and boards of directors must strive to produce profits for shareholders or they may get replaced. Therefore: either you manage constraints or they manage you. The constraints will determine the output of the system whether they are acknowledged and managed or not. The acknowledgment of these patterns is the ability to recognize the pattern.

The goal is to find a way of viewing how well a company is managing its TOC patterns through the "eyes" of their economic reports. Given the fact that economic reports are numbers reported by management, in a historical perspective they may not always reflect new strategies or changes in direction that the company is currently embarking upon, which would change the historical pattern. One extraordinary benefit of the Thinking Processes based on TOC and Economic Root Cause Analysis is that process provides the ability to recognize shifting patterns in the marketplace. Patterns are not definitive answers or de facto statements but are indicators, trends and directions as to movement in the marketplace and the company. Patterns should raise questions that in turn should stimulate action. TOC is the set of tools that assists in analyzing and recognizing patterns, raising questions and taking necessary action steps.

Pattern recognition is critical to knowing when the correct time occurs to make the necessary change. We cannot constantly monitor every assumption to be sure we are in line with constantly evolving reality, so the ability to spot the shifts can be a real advantage. Those who continue their old patterns of operation, regardless of the changing reality, will suffer when the effects of their actions are not those that they expect.

The Theory of Constraints as expressed in the Thinking Processes is a tool, not the only tool you have in the toolbox, but an important tool to help avoid being in the wrong place at the wrong time when market and economic patterns around us shift. Using TOC Thinking Processes and your insights, intuition and personal knowledge, guided by wisdom will help to:

- Recognize a profit decline. Especially when the current operating model of the business and/or industry matures or changes.

- Recognize and Focus on activities that show patterns of generating new profits and cash flow.

TOC defines three operational measurements that are key for investment pattern analysis. These three measurements should be viewed and analyzed as to whether the company being considered for investment is working toward these goal patterns. These three, as stated earlier, are the building blocks for emerging secondary patterns. The three measurements are:

Throughput (T): The <u>rate</u> at which the enterprise generates money through <u>sales</u>. In the world of "The Street" this is considered to be the same as Contribution Margin (selling price -- cost of raw materials). Labor costs are considered to be part of Operating Expense rather than throughput.

Inventory (I): All the money the enterprise invests in things, items it intends to (or could or wishes to) sell. This is the <u>total enterprise investment</u>, which includes conventional inventory, but also buildings, land, vehicles, plant, and equipment. Note: It does not include the value of labor added to Work-In-Process inventory.

Operating Expense (OE): All the money the system spends in turning Inventory into Throughput. This includes all of the money allocated to be put into an enterprise to keep it operating, such as heat, light, scrap materials, travel, entertainment, donations, marketing, public relations, R&D, training and education, benefits depreciation, all labor expenses even in the manufacturing sector which traditionally places labor as cost of goods.

So we are examining Three Primary Patterns: Throughput Patterns; Inventory Patterns and Operating Expense Patterns.

The following four measurements are incorporated into the patterns to identify results for the overall enterprise, which incorporates or blends with the basic principles of the Three Primary Measurements:

Net Profit = Throughput - Operating Expense (NP=T-OE)

Return on Investment (ROI) = (Throughput - Operating Expense) / Inventory

Productivity = Throughput / Operating Expense

With the TOC based economic and operational patterns in the TOC Pattern CD, investors can make assumptions and see patterns shifting and moving by examining the effect of those shifts and movements on the enterprises, overall Throughput, Inventory, and Operating Expense Pattern in addition to the Goal Patterns. A pattern that graphs out showing increasing overall Throughput, decreasing the overall Inventory, and/or decreasing the overall Operating Expense for the enterprise will generally be a good pattern for the business. This could be indicative of a company understanding where the patterns are shifting and moving, and thus taking advantage of the know-how and working knowledge of the management team and employees. The key here is recognizing the increase in Throughput patterns, while decreasing Inventory and/or Operating Expenses patterns. We too often see companies decreasing inventory and operating expenses because the throughput is dramatically taking a nosedive.

What can TOC Patterns help you look for!

As we stated earlier, it is important to look for the trend or pattern in the aggregation of the traditional reporting numbers. For instance, rapid throughput/sales accompanied by dramatic slowing in inventory and receivables turnover may indicate a pattern called "channel stuffing," bad credit quality of customers or poor credit quality on the customers. Companies anxious to hit extremely aggressive Wall Street expectations may ease credit policies, or get customers to accept too much product in return for easy credit. Companies might also perform services over a period of time of more than one quarter and have payment advanced. This robs from future quarters and suggests Throughput is not all it's cracked up to be in the view of traditional "street" analysis. If the economy slows, the company may get caught with substantial amounts of unsold in-process inventory, for which prices have plummeted.

TOC Asset Quality: What to look for as a Pattern

In addition to turnover of receivables and inventory, one should look for "capitalized expenses." Capitalization involves booking as an asset rather than an expense, costs of products or assets where revenues are expected to be realized over time. What does this mean in TOC patterns? It means what is and should be classified as OE is now being placed into the category I for inventory. Remember in viewing public information on companies the "balance sheet" for all practical purposes (give or take a tweak here and there) is the I (inventory) category in the tool box of TOC. In an attempt to match revenues and expenses, it is deemed appropriate in the world of publicly traded companies not to expense software development for which there is no current revenue possibility, even if there is a demonstrable ultimate market once completed. Once the software is finished and saleable, the company will begin to amortize (expense) the capitalized cost over the time of its expected economic usefulness. Capitalization of certain expenses can lead to assets of dubious quality and liquidity where ultimate realization is subject to realistic concern. You need to factor this reality into your examination of the numbers and establishing the patterns of the enterprise you are reviewing. This is very important with companies that have innovation as its core.

Computer companies capitalize software development. Retailers capitalize pre-opening expenses. So do restaurants. Companies capitalize software development they undertake. However, there are times when the software doesn't work and must be abandoned and written off. These assets may be of very dubious quality, and they may be written off, leading to so-called "one time" write-offs. Some companies engage in a "one time" write-off as a normal course of business. Unless you adjust for this in the models, your OE and I patterns may be skewed.

Channel Stuffing is found more often in technology related companies. Companies can be frantic to meet sales and earnings targets that they promised analysts over the past several quarters and may "stuff the channel" by giving tremendous economic terms to their retail outlets or other sales channels like Value Added Resellers (VARS). Watching and monitoring the receivables and inventory turns and the Productivity ratio will give you the red flags in these pattern movements. "The Street" may not see this deterioration in turnover so their customers may take severe losses. Keep in mind; channel stuffing robs from subsequent quarters to feed the current quarter. When management gets into this mode one of two things happen. One, Throughput unexpectedly accelerates and/or takes down the entire product from the channel. Two, the bluff is called and the stock implodes. Generally, it is the latter that occurs. Watch for this by monitoring the Inventory and Throughput patterns.

The TOC Value Creation adjustments have four major objectives and are compatible with common "Street" reporting models:

1. Move from an accrual basis to a cash basis to arrive at the correct timing of expenditure----for example accrual of bad debt reserve vs. write-off of bad debts.

2. Remove the impact of one-time events---work stoppages; gain on sale of securities, including the assets used in OE or I.

3. Remove the effect of debt financing and become a fully equity financed entity----need to deal with the tax situation of interest expenses in the annual statements.

4. Move from an accounting life of an asset to an economic life---increase or decrease the asset life of machinery, buildings, etc. to gain a true TOC pattern perspective.

The TOC measurements are incorporated into Pattern Models and are found in two major categories:

1. Economic accounting adjustments to restate generally accepted principles.

2. Adjustments to account for the one-time events in the life of a company, including environmental remediation, structuring, unusual gains and losses and work stoppages.

The underlying pattern for the TOC Value Creation adjustments to GAAP economics is to isolate the issues that management can control and to tie it to their policies, measurements and behaviors (PMBs) which is what the TOC way of analysis says will move a company to better economic strength in realizing the goal of the company. So what do we end up with? An adjusted net profit and asset base for ROI calculations. It is that simple.

The KEY to successfully linking TOC Value Creation to the "Street" for this analysis is to be certain that TOC Value Patterns are not allowed to be driven any lower than the top-line consolidated measurements of the economic reports. If the measures are driven any lower, to division or plants or departments, then micromanaging the links will quickly emerge and the patterns won't work on the analysis of economic statements for investment purposes. Keep in mind we are analyzing the whole company, not its parts.

Return on Investment (ROI) = Net Profit/Investment base

From this equation it should be easy to extrapolate the effect-cause-effect on ROI from the different changes in the profit equation or the investment base.

So what we are saying then, is that TOC Value can be summed up simply in two words: Focus and Leverage for the investor. The pattern will show where and how management is focusing resources to leverage ROI. Is the focus on Expanding markets and retaining customers? Improving operations? The leverage point should be continuously monitored and its status communicated by the models we have developed. A side benefit that we believe will come out of this model is that the patterns will show a need for the enterprise to create and become a continuous *learning* organization.

What Does "TOC Value" Mean?

TOC Value is Today's Value. The here and now. The "street" will call this "Present Value" to a greater or lesser degree. This now becomes the essence of the "Now Economy." TOC Value is "the value today of today's cash flow to grow tomorrow's cash stream." A dollar today is worth more than a dollar in the future, because you invest today's dollar and earn a positive rate of return, a process called compounding. The reverse of compounding is discounting, which converts a future cash flow into its equivalent present value.

How Do We Calculate TOC Value?

Let's look at a term called "free cash flow." This term Free Cash

Flow, and Cash Flow, are applicable in both public and private companies. The folks at the CNBC website (www.cnbc.com) give this definition of "free cash flow":

"This is cash flow from operations minus capital expenditures minus cash dividends paid -- at least in the view of some analysts. The truth is that opinions differ about what constitutes 'free' cash flow and how -- or whether -- it differs from conventional cash flow. The premise behind backing out capital expenditures and dividends is that these are optional and therefore should be set aside to see how much income a company is really generating. The dividend could always be suspended, after all, and even capital-intensive firms can usually limp along for a while on reduced capital outlays. The goal is the same as with cash flow: to look behind the smoke and mirrors sometimes associated with net income." *Website: www.CNBC.com*

The TOC patterns will help you "to look behind the smoke and mirrors" when monitoring throughput patterns.

For traditional Cash Flow you need to look at three factors that govern the present value of any given cash flow:

1. *How large is the cash flow?* The larger the cash flow, the larger the present value pattern.

2. *How risky is that cash flow?* As patterns may shift negatively, the investor expecting to receive a future cash flow from the business has to assume more risk--which lowers the value that you should pay today for that future cash flow. "Risk" is measured by the rate of return that you would require from an alternative investment that would generate a cash flow with the same level of risk.

3. *How long do we have to wait for the cash to start flowing?* The longer you have to wait, the less valuable the future cash flow. The length of the wait--the "Number of Years"--lowers the present value of a cash flow for two reasons. First, you could always invest that money in alternative investments that would earn interest during those years. Second, if you're not 100% confident that you will indeed get that cash flow, the more time that passes, the more risk you will have to assume--

which lowers the value that someone would pay today for that future cash flow.

The formula for calculating present value is:

Present Value = Future Cash Flow / (1 + Required Rate of Return) Number of years to wait for the cash to flow.

An Example of a Cash Flow Calculation

Net Present Value (NPV)

NPV helps us weigh the investment we are thinking about making against its return in what we call the discounted cash. The basic formula used for NPV is as follows:

NPV = Discounted incoming cash flows (we call this Revenue) minus any outgoing cash flow (investment) at the beginning.

Let's assume your friend comes to you and says he would like you to invest in his new startup business. The Opportunity will only be $4,000 in value today. Now you think, what can I get in return? Your friend says to you that he will return to you $1,000 per year for 5 years for your investment, and at the end of the 5th year will have given you back your investment. So you call your friendly local bank and ask what the current rates are for 5 years of borrowing money to enable you to do your comparison. The bank tells you the rate is 4%.

Do you do it? The answer can be found when you do the comparison.

Investment equals $5,000

Revenues (incoming Cash Flow)

        Year 1: $1,000 X .962 = $962

        Year 2: $1,000 X .925 = $925

        Year 3: $1,000 X .889 = $889

        Year 4: $1,000 X .855 = $855

Year 5: $1,000 X .822 = $822

TOTAL $4,453 (Discounted)

What we have is $4,453 in discounted income minus your initial investment of $5,000 equals $547. This is your NPV number.

Generally speaking people choose the positive figure. In choosing between several investment options your first selection would be the higher NPV, in our example that would be the $547. What you do need to consider in all investments is the amount of RISK that your investment is subject too. When looking at companies we believe one way to analyze the risk factor is to look at the patterns in the company.

Free Cash Flow

As stated earlier, one of the three main goals of corporations is to make more money--more profits--now and in the future; the next main goal is to have satisfied customers and the third is to have happy and empowered employees. So how does a corporation make money? Make Profits? Make Cash? It makes money by operating a business or series of businesses where it manufactures products or provides services. A company generates throughput by selling its products and services to and through the supply/service chain. In generating throughput, a company incurs expenses— salaries, cost of goods sold (CGS), selling and general administrative expenses (SGA), research and development (R&D) and so forth. The difference between operating throughput and operating expense is *Operating Income or Net Operating Profit.*

To produce throughput a corporation not only incurs operating expenses, but it also must invest money in inventory, real estate, buildings and equipment, and cash as working capital to support its business activities by converting inventory into throughput. The amount of cash that's left over after the payment of these investments and taxes is known as *Free Cash* flow to the company.

Free Cash Flow should be an important measure to stockholders and management. This is the cash that is left over after the payment of all cash expenses and operating investment required by the company. It is the cash that is available to pay the company's various claim holders, especially the good guys—the stockholders! The simple equation used to calculate Free Cash Flow is:

*Free Cash Flow = NOP (*Net Operating Profit) *minus Taxes minus Net Investment minus Net Change in Working Capital*

Free Cash Flow is the amount of cash that remains after deducting the funds the company must commit to continue operating at its planned level. If free cash flow is positive, then the company has met all of its planned cash commitments and has cash available to reduce debt or expand; if free cash flow is negative, the company will have to take actions, such as selling investments, raising more cash from investors, borrowing money, or issuing stock in the short term to continue at the same level that the company's operating plan calls for.

Cash Flow Verses Profit

Profit and cash flow are two entirely different entities, yet many people often think the two are the same or just a different expression of each other. Profit and cash flow are different, each with entirely different results as they relate to Throughput. The concept of profit is somewhat broad and only looks at income and expenses over a certain period of time; if you are an analyst on Wall Street you may be only concerned with a period of time that is quarter to quarter. Profit is an interest concept in the modern business world for calculating your federal and state taxes.

Cash flow, on the other hand, is a very dynamic tool focusing on the day-to-day operations of a business owner. It is the lifeblood that flows through the company's veins and allows the business to convert inventory into throughput. Cash flow is concerned with the flow of money in and out of a business. But more importantly, it is concerned with the times at which the flow of the money takes place. Having sufficient Free Cash Flow in a business is essential for achieving the goal of the company. Without cash flow a business will be limited in its efforts to expand markets and retain customers. If it can't expand markets and retain customers then the company will be forced to downsize its operations.

Theoretically a company that is profitable can find itself in bankruptcy court. This would truly be contrary to the principles of TOC and common sense. Can this happen? It would take a lot of negligence in managing cash flow, but it could happen. Look at any business and look at the difference between profit and cash flow and how they relate. For example, if a retail business bought a $1000 item and turned around to sell it for $2000, then you have made a $1000 profit. But what if the buyer of the item is slow to pay his or her bill, and six months pass before you collect on the account? Your retail business may still show a profit, but what about the bills it has to pay during that six-month period? You may not have the cash to pay the bills despite the profits you earned on the sale. Furthermore this cash flow gap may cause you to miss other profit opportunities, damage your credit rating, and force you to take out loans and create debt.

Warren Buffett recently has told his shareholders of Berkshire Hathaway that his method of valuing a company is based on the saying: "a bird in the hand is worth two in the bush."

As Buffett suggests: "To flesh out this principle, you must answer only three questions. How certain are you that there are indeed birds in the bush? When will they emerge and how many will there be? What is the risk-free interest rate? ... If you can answer these three questions, you will know the maximum value of the bush and the maximum number of the birds you now possess that should be offered for it." *Berkshire Hathaway website for 1999 annual report.*

What Warren Buffett is describing is pattern recognition and movement.

In applying the wisdom of Warren Buffett, investors face a variety of models and methods. We are providing an overview of a method of valuation based on patterns in a company that may give you insights into whether or not there are birds in the bush and how many birds there may be in the bush.

The economics philosophy of TOC thereby tells us to look to "The Statement of Sources and Uses of Working Capital" as the key to a company being managed accordingly to the principles of TOC. We need to examine the sources of funds and uses of funds to know if the company is moving in the direction of increasing

Throughput, and decreasing inventory and operating expenses. The "Statement of Cash Flow" is critical, this is the "minds-eye" of TOC economics and finance, and this "minds-eye" is what separates those focused on the goal of the company versus just trying to make the EPS number look good for the analyst on the street. Look at how a company is sourcing its working capital requirements and capital expenditures, and we learn a great deal about the philosophy of the management and board of the company.

The company that is managing its business in accordance with TOC principles, whether it knows anything about TOC or not, will be thinking Customer Back and not the Company Forward. Such a company will recognize customer patterns that change, and which will trigger a change in operations and processes creating new opportunities for new business patterns. Traditional investors often ignore companies that manage their business in congruence with TOC concepts because they can't see the pattern movement.

Understanding customer patterns means knowing as much about the customer as the company knows about itself. This is a level of customer relationship that goes beyond saying I have sales reps who have relationships with purchasing agents. It means the company understands the economics of their supply chain, the functionality of the supply chain and the value of the customer in the entire enterprise model in a real time mode of operation. When a company functions this way you will see their throughput pattern movement on the rise and the inventory and operating expense levels remain constant or proportionate to throughput. The company is then on the road to expanding its markets, retaining its customers and improving the overall operations of the enterprise.

CHAPTER FOUR
Taking the Voodoo Out of Company Analysis

"Buying a stock the way you would buy a house. Understand it and like it such that you'd be content to own it in the absence of any market"

—*Warren Buffett*

To develop the concept of TOC Patterns, this chapter looks at the following points and questions:

- Key variables in assessing economic information that is relevant to reporting required by government agencies, and economic information that is necessary for understanding pattern movements. How can we bridge this gap?
- How do we define a pattern? Define the company to be analyzed?
- Which pattern triggers—sales, operating costs, and free cash flow, operating leverage, cost efficiencies, and inventory efficiencies?
- Which throughput pattern factors affect which operating expense value drivers?
- What key line items in reports comprise what patterns?

The Essential Ideas

- To earn consistent returns, you must improve your ability to recognize shifting patterns in market movements.
- The patterns—which stem from traditional value triggers, should help you to visualize the causes and effects of TOC pattern movement.
- Throughput growth with adequate Free Cash Flow is your most likely source of investment opportunities.

- *"Think customer back not company forward."* This is a pattern that is at the heart of any company that is living a process of ongoing improvement through innovation.
- When looking for value through growth, it is clear that you should look at companies that focus first on their customers, not on their internal silos, when determining internal success factors.
- When doing investment analysis one should look at a company and determine from the data if value is flowing in or out of the company. Do the operations and marketing plans demonstrate a sense of stability?

Company Analysis

Learning to see strategic patterns can help managers identify the next "profit zone" ahead of competitors and, ultimately, create a business design that will tap the latent value there. Numerous companies are testaments to the tremendous shareholder value that can be generated by seeing tomorrow's profit zone today. But how do you do it? In an economy characterized by information overload, merely searching is not enough; you will be inundated with information, with conflicting observations, with evidence of all types. Instead, you need to keep an eye out for three categories of "pattern leading indicators": dysfunctional, variability, and a shift in the direction or rate of change. The presence of any of these conditions suggests that one or more new patterns may emerge. Small-business customers, who traditionally have been poorly served by suppliers because they haven't generated huge profits, provide a good testing ground for pattern thinking and methods.

Business Cycle

What TOC economics refer to, as a Business Cycle, is a recurring pattern of expansion and contraction in the economy. The average cycle is 3 to 4 years. TOC economics believe that by monitoring certain patterns you can anticipate the movement and adjust accordingly. The famous hockey player Greztke always said he "saw the pattern on the ice and skated to where he knew the puck would go." One needs to understand that the business cycle or pattern is the recurring pattern of expansion and contraction (recession) of the economy. Economists will generally say the economy usually expands for 3 or more years of economic growth, and then contracts for 1 to 2 years (recession). In the 1980s the expansion lasted much longer than expected and in the early 1990s, the recession lasted longer than expected.

Patterns and their Movement

With rare exception, today's business is structured in a way that each of its different parts (each department, function, cost center, business unit.) is induced to operate, almost exclusively, as if an independent entity. Each part is managed according to its own "bottom line," its own strategic and tactical plans, its own budget and plans for using it, its own policies, measurements and/or procedures - most of these having been created in isolation, without taking into account their impact on the other parts, or the organization as a whole. No wonder it's so common to find parts of an organization in conflict with others, improvement projects geared to profitability rarely achieving their intended benefits, organizations disenchanted with empowering their people and spending exorbitant amounts of financial resources teaching their employees conflict resolution - with seemingly little impact!

We believe if you see companies managing themselves as if they are composed of independent parts, each taking its own direction and ignoring their inherent connectedness to the whole company, they will never be able to effectively move in positive patterns consistently and become a business that is focused on continuous improvement. The kind of continuous improvement that makes investing stable and ongoing.

Unlike most stock and company analysis programs and efforts, TOC Pattern Movement Analysis provides organizations with a more common sense view and method that enables you to look at the parts of an organization to synchronize them around achieving the greatest benefit for the organization as a whole: to focus on *global* pattern movement based on TOC-derived performance attributes, rather than traditional "street" performance analysis.

We have developed a series of focus management areas to look at for movement from quarter to quarter. These four areas provide insight into how the common sense attributes of TOC and normal economic reporting can be applied to bringing an understanding of an organization and its performance in the marketplace. Each of these economic views provides the insight needed by the different parts to synchronize their activities as one. This approach is called TOC Pattern Analysis. The process that underlies the TOC patterns is simple, logical and rigorous, answering three questions: (1) What to change? (2) What to change to? (3) How to cause a change? When you look at the pattern movement of economic trends in a business and see movements down or flat, invoke the three questions regarding the trend and the company. In doing your research on the company find out if they recognize patterns and are able to answer the three questions.

Start to think in terms of asking questions; questions that apply to the company you are analyzing and ask:

What to change – what is happening, what are the patterns and what must change to thrive and survive?
What to change to – what are the enabled business capabilities needed to make this company successful and what do those patterns look like? Can the company be successful?
How to change – how does the company create the capabilities to succeed and continually change?

The catalyst, which drives patterns, should be the continuum, which drives the entire economic life cycle of the company.

There are various questions that an investor needs to ask relative to operations and patterns that may be difficult to ascertain from financial data. We believe it is important for all serious investors to sit in on "earnings calls" that all publicly traded companies do at least quarterly and pose questions to the management team regarding strategy, marketing, management beliefs and implementation of corporate objectives. If you are working with a broker, have the broker answer your questions based on the research that the firm he/she represents conducts on companies they promote.

Questions that are important and will have an influence on the pattern models are:

- Technology/Systems: are there any new breakthroughs the company is looking at that will assist in increasing throughput, expanding markets and retaining customers? Don't let who ever answers the question steer away from the question by re-directing the answer to technology that reduces overhead and cost. This understanding of technology as a cost driver is common knowledge, over used and over-emphasized in most companies. The real benefits of breakthrough technology are to increase throughput, technology that will drive market share and expand the customer base.
- What does this company see as the next real operational breakthrough over the next three to five years that will expand markets, improve operations and retain customers?
- Does this company see a role in using or engaging technology or processes that will lead to breakthrough market conditions?
- Does the company use and own technology long enough to cause growth to happen?
- Who really manages the technology? Is technology management core to the business?
- Does this company understand how customers are changing? Do they understand the demographics of their customers whether that is a business-to-business customer or a consumer customer?
- Do the profit drivers of the company match in any way with the patterns you are monitoring?
- Does this company demonstrate a basis for differentiation from their competitors? Can you relate to that differentiation? Does this company give you as a consumer of products or services a "good feeling"? Would you buy? Would you use the services? Do they have a unique value position that drives throughput?
- Is R&D internal or outsourced? Does this company focus on process or product? Can it tell the difference? Can the company explain it to you in "layperson" language or do they use complicated phrases and an endless series of subordinated clauses in explaining the answer. How does this company manage its portfolio of R&D?
- What is the "go to market strategy?" How is it implemented? What is the turnover rate of the sales force, account managers, business development managers and executives associated

with throughput? How often does the go to market strategy change?
- What are the company's most important strategies and priorities? Do they link with the patterns that you are monitoring? Can they name their top three priorities for the year? Can they demonstrate the cause/effect of making those priorities a reality?
- What are the company's economic assumptions that they are designing their strategy around? Do competitors have similar assumptions?
- What element of the business design/plan is linked to the priorities that you believe are important for success as an investment?
- How long will the business plan be sustainable? What will change to make it sustainable? Do the answers link to your patterns that you are monitoring?
- What are the cycles for this company? For the industry that this company competes within? Can you map those cycles to historical data and trends?
- Can you tell where in the life cycle this company is living?
Is this a company that can be or will be affected by Real Time Enterprises and Zero Latency Enterprises? Does this company understand what Real Time Enterprises are all about?
- Are there plans to consider the effects of a Real Time Enterprises environment within this company?
- The supply chain or service chain that this company operates within has certain attributes. Do you understand them? Does the company you are investing in understand those attributes?

The key question posed in the use of pattern movements is: "Where will the company be next year as a profit making company in their industry and/or supply chain?" Our contention is that something has happened to the way the world does business, and the result is that the verities of strategy of 20 years ago don't apply anymore. And our assertion is that the most dangerous thing you can do as a business is to keep doing business in the old way of doing things, as opposed to migrating with, or in advance of, the customer. Certain Patterns speak to us about the realization of the operational strategy of the business. Think of TOC Economic

Patterns as a tool for linking business, patterns and the investor as one.

TOC patterns comprise two simple ideas: (1) you can study a company and estimate the growth and profitability that the analyst and PR media data presents to you, or (2) you will be a more informed and astute observer of business growth and profitability if you correctly anticipate movement in patterns that have a direct correlation to those price-implied expectations that the company is always telling you about in their analyst calls.

The "street" values stocks using the discounted cash flow model, and so we'll use it along with TOC economic patterns we have compiled to better understand movements towards or away from the goal of the company. The basic operating value drivers are sales growth, operating profit margin, and investment. In analyzing TOC Patterns we need to be concerned with two fundamental questions:

1. Where should we look for TOC Patterns?

Let's take a closer look at a pattern that is common to all investors. The Bear Market. Most economists will tell us that a bear market precedes a recession. The market (The Street) discounts (anticipates and begins reacting to) future events. Analysts try to see a coming slowdown by watching pattern movement in a bear pattern such as:

- Decreasing backlogs on orders for durable and consumer goods. *(Effects throughput & Inventory)*

- Decreasing plant utilization. Lay-offs and early retirements *(effects Inventory & Operating Expense)*

- Decreasing auto and steel output. *(This is a supply chain cause-effect issue)*

- Decreasing auto and home sales and appliances. *(This is a supply chain cause-effect issue)*

- Decreasing housing starts. *(This is a supply chain cause-effect issue)*

- Increasing unemployment claims. *(This is a supply chain cause-effect issue)*

- Increasing inflation or interest rates. *(This is a supply chain cause-effect issue)*

- Decrease in the use of consultants in large corporations. *(This is a supply chain cause-effect issue)*

2. Are all patterns and economic information created equally?

Realize that when a supply chain cause-effect issue impacts the company's throughput, there will always be an impact on inventory and operating expenses. All of this affects value. As you monitor the trends in the market and the industry, map the cause/effect to the TOC patterns for the company being monitored. Do you notice a shift in patterns? Is there disintegration of the supply chain? Are the throughput channels being compressed? Is there convergence? Competitors are all looking alike and what effect does this have on the buying strategy of the consumer or B2B buyer?

The answers are important because they tell us something about the starting point, the mid-point and ending point in the search for knowledge about the goal of the company. Using the principles of TOC and elements of pattern theory we are able to assemble TOC based economic patterns to better monitor trends and movements of a company based on economic data provided by the company. Knowing today's stock price of a company by reading the morning paper is one thing, but knowing where that company is headed and the impact that direction will have on the value of the company in the future is another important consideration. This tells us that not all patterns are created equally. "Buyer Beware." Do your homework.

We are looking at certain patterns. Not all items in the pattern may be relevant to all companies at all times. Some items may not be easily found in all reports. Some items will be more relevant than others depending on markets and industries. Over all we believe the following patterns and their components speak to us as investors as to movements, operational strategies of the company and leadership thereof. Hence there are ample items in each pattern that if one item is missing, or if another is not relevant, the pattern movement and trend is still identifiable. What we have attempted to do is identify as close as possible standard reporting items that in and of themselves possess the policies, measurements and behaviors of the "spirit" of what TOC considers to be "ongoing process improvement" of achieving the goal of profit-making companies. Realize that line items in economic reports comprise elements that may not be found in other company's reports. But the pattern movement over a period of time often is the same movement with or without those few elements that are contained or missing in the line items from a TOC perspective only.

Pattern - THROUGHPUT ITEMS
Total Sales in nominal and real dollars (T)
Sales Growth (T)
Profit Growth (T)
Profit Margin (T)

Pattern - THROUGHPUT PATTERNS
Sales per employee in nominal and real dollars (T&OE)
Profit per employee in nominal annual dollars (T& OE)
Selling, general, and administrative expenses as a percent of sales (OE)
Research and development as a percent of sales (OE RATE)
Collection period in days (OE RATE)

Pattern - INVENTORY ITEMS
PP&E (property plant and equipment) (I)
Balance Sheet number (I)
Inventory turnover ratio (I)
Return on Equity (I)
Return on Assets (I)

Pattern - INVENTORY PATTERNS
Ratio of Debt to equity (I & OE RATE)
Ratio of long term debt to equity (I & OE RATE)

Interest expense as a percent of sales (OE RATE)

Pattern - THE RATIOS OF THE GOAL
High Stock price to earnings per share
Low stock price to earnings per share
Average stock price to earnings per share
FREE CASH FLOW/Share
Free CASH FLOW
Return on Sales
Dividend payout ratio

The TOC Pattern Model

Where did all that value go, and why did it go there? Questions we may ask from time to time about our investments and the companies they are made of. All too often we do not think of our investments as the company we are investing in but as the "representative" of our investment.

We created the Models to help you distinguish in conjunction with your other investment tools where individual companies are moving along the pattern roadmap towards the goal of the company. Unlike most investment analysis tools, the TOC Pattern Analysis Approach provides investors with a common sense view of economic data as it relates to trends and patterns in the operational aspects of the business. It is not a tool to calculate today's buy or sell stock price. It is a model that enables the parts of an organization to synchronize the patterns around achieving the greatest benefit for the organization as a whole; to focus on global performance, rather than local performance; to understand the patterns that help managers lead to success and achieve the goals of the company.

Having the insight into *what* is required is only part of the solution. Two absolutely necessary conditions for success are for the entire company to have this same insight and to reach across-the-board consensus on precisely how to proceed.

The TOC Pattern Management Approach

Just as a physician diagnosing the disease causing many of a patient's symptoms, TOC and your other key investment analysis tools will aid you in using the cause and effect thinking processes to identify and reach consensus on the core problem facing investors: why are some of my investments not moving as desired? People intuitively understand the futility of fighting symptoms; once you know the pattern movement and if all signs indicate a negative or declining trend over time you can assume there is a core problem.

Companies boost their value growth three ways: by boosting their revenue profit growth (Throughput), by reducing their assets (Inventory) and cost (Operating Expenses), and through differentiation and strategic control by effectively using business process, people and technology. All three ideas are aspects of business design, and business design is the real theme of the TOC Pattern approach. But investors don't get a lot of chances. Knowledge of how a company operates is not always available the way it is available to insiders. How important is business design and Patterns? Very!! If the myth of the old verities was "Managers need more relevant information," the new reality is "Managers need accurate models."

What we do in TOC economics by means of analysis is to spot problems and patterns that may not be broadly recognized by what you read in the press, hear or view on the radio and TV, or for that matter what is put in the companies' web pages.

As you saw in chapter two, "Economics" is considered and viewed as the "theoretical" cousin of accounting and finance. In most cases, economics is regarded as a more "practical discipline" than accounting. The world of economics comprises more than finance and accounting information. It incorporates the study of human behavior as it relates to the use, consumption and utilization of money, people, ideas, inventory and goals to satisfy the needs and wants of the company, the investors and the marketplace. Economics is always focused on the "methods" of organizing the world of production, how the goods get distributed and the marketplace consumption of goods and services.

Economic and TOC Financial Analysis probes the Balance Sheet, the Income Statement, and the Statement of Sources and Uses of Working Capital from three basic premises: Is Throughput increasing? Is Inventory going down or staying the same? And is the company becoming more efficient? Keep in mind that if inventory stays level and operating expenses stay level and the only movement is in the increase of Throughput, this is a good pattern. The economic pattern is that the company has learned how to increase the rate of sales, possibly expand their markets and retain their customers without increasing the cost factors of the company.

The Balance Sheet is a point in time view of Assets and Liabilities and Shareholder's Equity (derived by subtracting liabilities from assets). This should always be viewed as a pattern. Look to understanding the Balance sheet over consecutive 8 quarters or over several years. Do not just view the balance sheet as a one-quarter "on the spot" decision maker for pattern movement.

The Income Statement as reported by most companies whether they are public or private shows the results of monthly operations including revenues, less the cost of goods sold, operating expenses, non-cash charges, interest expenses, and taxes and so forth. When viewing the Income Statement with the "minds-eye" of TOC economics, we discover that the Income Statement incorporates most of the T- I - OE concerns collectively, and sometimes the elements are blended. The blended elements require one to do more research in either separating the elements or creating some compensating algorithm to better understand the pattern. This compensating and/or adjusting are often needed to fully understand how the Income statement is being compiled to make sure we are viewing the economic patterns of TOC.

When reading corporate documents and reports you will undoubtedly come across various categories of ratios and financial data that are reported because it represents the "common language" of accounting. Remember companies report in accounting language not in terms of an economic viewpoint. Let us take a look at some of the more common categories that one will find and what they may mean to the economics of TOC.

Depreciation

Depreciation is the accounting procedure, which allocates the cost of a fixed asset over its useful life.

Depreciation is one of the most confusing aspects of accounting, Most people believe that if we did not have to pay taxes in the current system no one would give a hoot about depreciation. Sometimes, because of inflation or other external factors, the actual open-market value of a building will increase with age rather than decrease. Most people assume that will happen with the house they live in. But most business capital investments, like machinery, computers, furniture or manufacturing plants as a whole, do indeed wear out and lose value. In any event, accountants have a tendency to ignore market values. The IRS tells you in great detail just how much to depreciate any kind of asset during each year of its life—buildings, automobiles, trucks, appliances, farm machinery, bulldozers, etc. So market values have nothing to do with it. You realize tax savings (or at least tax deferments) by deducting depreciation losses. You must deduct them in any event. Even if you do not, the IRS will tax you the same as if you did! In the world of TOC accounting they will make adjustments in the OE view and Inventory view regarding depreciation. In our work we found this distinction in TOC accounting not having a significant effect on the Inventory patterns of the company from an economic perspective. The economic value pattern over a period of time reflected the same pattern movement regardless of the TOC accounting adjustment for inventory and depreciation.

Liquidity Ratios

Many companies provide the liquidity ratios on their website or in their reports. From a TOC economic perspective they should be used with the pattern analysis in determining movement in the three main TOC patterns of T – I – OE. Liquidity ratios determine how well the company can satisfy maturing short-term debt obligations. This can be important when assessing how safe a stock is as an investment. Liquidity ratios are concerned with obligations that are due within one year. This will impact OE.

Current Ratio - The working capital or ratio of Current Assets (assets maturing within one year of statement date) divided by Current Liabilities (liabilities maturing within one year of the statement date). Current Assets generally consist of Cash, Marketable Investments maturing within one year, Current Receivables, and Inventory. Current Liabilities consist of Accounts Payable, Current Debt, and Deferred Income. Let's look at an example:

$$\textbf{Current Ratio} = \frac{\text{Current Assets: } \$900,000}{\text{Current Liabilities: } \$200,000} = 4.5*$$

*1.9 is industry average

What this is telling us is that the company is safer than its competitors by a wide margin. In the mind of a TOC economic analysis, the company may be in a very good position. But this may indicate that the OE pattern may be shifting downward over the course of the next several quarters even though the current analysis using the TOC patterns in a few quarters may indicate all is fine or getting better. This supports our belief that one needs to analyze the patterns of a company over 8 quarters as provided in the models and continue the analysis as a rolling forward model, adding the next quarter that is current and dropping the oldest quarter. This way you will be able to produce a rolling forward pattern movement. Sometimes when companies are in this position with this type of current ratio, they may decide to do investing in equipment or real estate, which will change the ratio in the quarters to come.

Quick Ratio - This is the ratio for measuring the short-term solvency questions. It is a ratio of Current Assets minus Inventory divided by Current Liabilities. This is a better measure of liquidity since the true nature of liquidity under duress is difficult to determine. Forced liquidations can lead to very disappointing realizations. A quick ratio higher than one is desirable. This is why many in the accounting arena refer to the Quick Ratio as the "acid test."

Let's look at an example:

$$\textbf{Quick Ratio} = \frac{\text{Cash/AR/Securities} - \text{Inventory: \$600,000}}{\text{Current Liabilities: \$200,000}} = 3*$$

*1.0 is industry average

Why is this important from a TOC economic perspective? Inventory can be turned to cash only through sales, so the quick ratio gives you a better picture of your ability to meet your short-term obligations, regardless of your sales levels. Over time, a stable current ratio with a declining quick ratio may indicate that you've built up too much inventory and explain why the graph in the model is showing an upper pattern movement for your inventory items. In the patterns of TOC economics one will want to see actions being taken by the company management in converting inventory to cash to improve this ratio. Which translates to mean increasing the Throughput.

When viewing the patterns and analyzing the current ratio and the quick ratio, one should keep in mind that they give only a "snapshot" of the business's ability to meet short-term obligations. They are not an indication of whether each specific obligation can be paid when due. To determine the likelihood of payment probability, you will need to construct a cash flow model or look at the Free Cash Flow patterns.

Receivables Turnover - Sales for the Period divided by Average Receivables (Beginning Receivables minus Ending Inventories divided by two.) The trend in this ratio is extremely important to determine credit quality of the customers. Are they really increasing Throughput by selling to people who pay their bills? Is the company meeting its deliverables? There are times companies will book sales even if customers have not accepted or received delivery.

Let's look at the formula:

$$\textbf{Receivables Turnover} = \frac{\text{Sales: \$4,000,000}}{\text{Average Receivables: \$3,500,000}} = 1.1*$$

*1.1 times is industry average

The pattern movement here may indicate that this company is not as successful in asset utilization as it is in profitability. Meaning it is not converting what they sell, as indicated in the throughput patterns, into cash for the goal of the company. The company does not collect its receivables (bills) as quickly as it should for TOC pattern movement but is at the industry average. By examining this item and comparing it to the TOC pattern you will be able to determine if this issue (used as an example) is just a "fluke" in the quarter or is contributing to the overall pattern movement of the company. Poor receivables turnover further complicates matters affecting Throughput in the future, if the company's customers have difficulty paying their bills, or stop paying their bills and go out of business. Recognizing these patterns and their movements will give you an indication of the company's ability to implement a process of ongoing improvement.

Total Asset Turnover - Trends in Total Asset Turnover (Sales for the Period divided by Average Total Assets for the period) can unearth dead assets if the ratio is deteriorating and there is no valid explanation. TOC economic patterns may indicate how efficient a company is in generating Throughput from the inventory that is being used to convert to sales. The higher the number, the more efficient the company. This then can be mapped to the pattern movement in the OE patterns.

$$\textbf{Total Asset Turnover} = \frac{\text{Sales: } \$400{,}000}{\text{Total Assets: } \$2{,}500{,}000} = .16*$$

*2.5 times is the industry average

It is important to look for the pattern in these numbers. For instance, rapid sales accompanied by radical slowing in inventory and receivables turnover may indicate channel stuffing, bad credit quality of customers or erroneous and premature booking of sales before customer acceptance. Companies sometimes are anxious to hit extremely aggressive Wall Street expectations as we have seen over and over again, and what they will do is ease their credit policies, or have their sales departments convince the customers to accept too much product in return for easy credit. This robs from future quarters and suggests growth is not all it's cracked up to be, and indicates that management is not focused on the true GOAL of the company, or what TOC defines as the GOAL. This can mean a real disaster in the making. Once Wall Street analysts are "spooked," it's tough to get them back in the recommending mode for the company.

Companies with substantial amounts of In-Process Inventory as opposed to Finished or Raw Inventory may have a lower quality of liquidity. If the economy slows, the company may get caught with substantial amounts of unsold in-process inventory, for which prices have plummeted. This is why these numbers in the world of TOC are all treated together as one Inventory number or pattern. They should be viewed as one set of patterns collectively.

Asset Quality - Debt Utilization Ratios

Debt utilization ratios measure how well the company is utilizing borrowed funds to make sure they can convert inventory into throughput. Debt funds OE in all respects. Debt buys Inventory. Knowing if the debt that is on the books and the company's ability to repay the debt are realistic will tell one how well management is working within the principles of a process of ongoing improvement towards the goal of the company. Novice investors and even some not so novice investors believe that a company with no debt is superior in operations to all other companies. Having little debt on the balance sheet is generally very safe and good. But most companies assume debt to finance operations (OE) so the company can grow and achieve the goal. General accounting textbooks state that the ideal ratio is around 30%. Due to the increase in leveraged buyout (LBO) activity amongst companies over the last 10 years the ratio of debt to assets or equity has been increasing. When analyzing the patterns of TOC economics one must take into consideration that items called Property, Plant, and Equipment and Capitalized Software Development Costs, to use the common language of accountants, are not recorded or treated as TOC Inventory items. They are capitalized when put into service or as the software is completed. These "long-term assets" are then depreciated or amortized over their expected "economic life" and hence recorded as an expense (OE). Obsolete property, or items that have no current value, specifically capitalized software that has gone nowhere either because it doesn't work or because the competition was superior in their selling efforts, will be written off by today's auditors and CFO's. So in the world of TOC economic patterns one will need to compensate and do some re-calculating on the asset side of the house to get a better picture of the movement. Also realize that many companies are, at times, hesitant to startle the Street with these write-off and write-downs. Often, these unproductive assets build up on the balance sheet until the auditors make an issue of them and force write-offs.

These assets when written off will be called "one time" write-offs. Watch for these items. Some companies engage in "one time" write-off as a normal course of business. It may appear as if they are doing one time write-off's every quarter or every other quarter. Look for the pattern in one time write-off's and ask questions as to why? This should invoke the question as to how well the company is managing in the framework of a process of ongoing improvement if they are engaging at will in write-offs. This will have an impact on the economic patterns of T - I - OE over one or two quarters. When doing the TOC analysis over eight quarters look for the pattern and recognize when the company may have taken the "write-offs" and in what quarter the write-off was taken, so proper TOC analysis of the patterns will be done and the adjustments made in your model, or at least realized in your mind.

Look for the following ratios in most reporting documents:

$$\textbf{Debt to Total Asset} = \frac{\text{Total Debt: } \$800,000}{\text{Total Assets: } \$2,500,000} = 32\%*$$

*32% is the industry norm

This company's debt to total assets is at the industry average. What does this mean? The company is not really leveraged. What you want to watch for is highly leveraged companies. The TOC economic pattern in highly leveraged companies usually indicates a company not focused on a process of ongoing improvement over the long haul. It could mean that management or the board or investors/owners have other motives.

Creating Earnings the TOC way – Companies that have earned or been accorded (there's a big difference) high P/E's (Price Earnings Ratio) can use this inexpensive currency to buy earnings.

Earnings Per Share

Net income divided by the number of common shares of stock outstanding.

If a company consistently retained 80 percent of its earnings and paid out the other 20 percent to the stockholders, you would see a pattern being developed that is goal oriented. Now you may say that is not enough return for me. Remember, however, that the company actually earned five times that much and kept the balance as retained earnings. If it is a well-managed company focused on the process of ongoing improvement, and a company that is expanding its markets, retaining its customers and improving the efficiencies by which they operate, you are probably better off having it retain 80 percent or more of the earnings for more growth next year instead of paying it out as dividends. It amounts to sort of an automatic tax-free reinvestment program; you will not pay taxes on the re-invested dollars, but you will pay taxes on any dividends paid out to you. (The company has already paid taxes on it once as part of their earnings, whether it paid out dividends or not. That's double taxation.) Warren Buffett prefers that companies he invests in pay no dividends. He would rather see the company re-invest all of its earnings, thereby growing the company faster, and avoiding any tax on dividend payouts.

Top line revenue growth that is much lower than bottom line growth can be a source of a future pattern that is not in harmony with the TOC GOAL or one of a process of ongoing improvement. This could suggest improper timing in expense recognition or it could suggest gross margin improvement, which is a result of huge write-downs in prior quarters.

It is important to diligently examine the patterns in gross and operating margins, to assess price competitiveness and the general cost of managing the business. If a company has to spend more to get its product into the market, at the same time gross margins are deteriorating, it could suggest deteriorating fundamentals or a pattern movement away from ongoing improvement.

Another negative is the merging of deteriorating unit volume growth and deteriorating pricing power, suggesting an industry with way too much capacity unless there is a huge pickup in demand. Many businesses exhibit these characteristics before serious declines in business fundamentals and stock price. The DRAM companies, PC manufacturers, restaurants, metal manufacturers, and manufacturers of computer memory have all demonstrated these issues. The stocks have suffered accordingly.

Leverage

We have mentioned the term leverage in the previous examples. The concept of leverage could be a good one or a bad one depending on the intent. Leverage back in the days of the real estate boom in the early and mid-80s, became the cause of many real estate failures in the late 80s and early 90s. The real estate failures gave rise to new "fortunes" that were focused on creating wealth in this market. Sam Zell was the king of real estate turnarounds. In the front yard of the Chicago office where Sam Zell crafted his turnaround art is a statue of a "grave dancer" with the following inscription:

> "If it's Santa you was 'specting
> Well you better get down
> Cause it's the Gravedancers Redux
> Who are coming to town.
>
> Who asked them to the party?
> It's pretty plain to see
> The lenders and the spenders
> Made them hop with glee.
>
> Leverage was the beverage
> That got this party cookin'
> But the hangover's set in
> And now a Gravedancer's lookin'
>
> It's Gravedancer times
> When there's panic in the land

> When assets sell at costs that scream,
> "Bail me out, Man!!"

Well the poem has "meaning" to those in the dot-com bust of 2000 and 2001 besides the real estate world of the late 80s. Leverage relates to the amount of debt incurred in relation to shareholder's equity, and suggests the amount of risk (losses) a business can withstand before it is incapable of covering its obligations. Basically how much cushion is there to "weather the storm"? Highly leveraged businesses that are cyclical and have earnings variability can have their status as a going concern severely jeopardized in market downturns. These are patterns that must be monitored. They are signs of patterns shifting away from the goal and the principles of an ongoing improvement methodology. High long-term debt does not go away just because the market or the patterns shift. If the throughput patterns shift and there are negative effects on the goal of the company, having high long-term debt will have adverse effects on the company. The pattern will begin to change and companies will begin to reduce operating expenses to compensate.

The TOC ratios that make the most sense in terms of the philosophy of the GOAL and T -I - OE principles are the following:

> Total Liabilities to Shareholder's Equity
> Debt to Shareholder's Equity
> Debt to Total Capital (Debt plus Equity)
> One of the most important in terms of TOC and one that is at the heart of TOC is called Free Cash Flow.

Free cash flow is a way to compare apples to oranges. Further, it is from this free cash flow that debt is really reduced or that money for strategic initiatives is derived.

A criticism of technology (espoused by Peter Lynch, amongst others) is that the technology industry never really generates free cash flow since it is constantly reinventing itself to avoid being outflanked. All cash flow must be plowed back into the business and much of the capitalized cost on the balance sheet may involve old useless technology, which should have accelerated write-offs or rates of amortization. You must look at the particulars of each company to draw the appropriate conclusion. This can be a difficult exercise. But a very worthwhile exercise to do in collaboration with the TOC pattern models. The bigger and more diversified the company, the more arduous the task in determining the true situation.

Ratios vary by industry and revolve around the nature of the assets, their liquidity, and the speed they turn over, and the degree to which the asset may have a special purpose. For example, the purchase of real estate for warehousing purposes because of rising demand in the product could be a special purpose. Often management may think it is good to spend money as long as the demand is there to support it, but if they did not determine whether the demand is ongoing or a fluke in the business cycle it will have an impact on the ratios going forward. The consistency or variability of profitability has a very important bearing on debt capacity.

Banks, because their assets are viewed as liquid and collectible, are leveraged at over 20 times (total liabilities to equity). Software companies, in many cases, have no debt. Drug companies, because they have substantial free cash flow, in many cases, have no debt.

Some companies believe judicious leverage augments Return of Equity and hence Earnings Per Share (Net Income divided by shares outstanding), as long as the Return on Assets exceeds the incremental cost of debt. However, there is a risk adjustment process where the market will markdown the Price Earnings Ratio (P/E) if the risk from debt appears to be thwarting needed initiatives or creating undue risk.

It is important to be knowledgeable of the risks of highly leveraged financial conditions, particularly in cyclical businesses. If there is a positive, it is that a highly leveraged business in a cyclical downturn, with no debt capacity or ability to sell equity, may have no choice but to sell to a competitor creating the opportunity for a quick pop in the troubled company's stock. This last possibility is not an investment strategy so much as a "redeeming" consideration.

Cash Flow Analysis

For those who have seen the movies called "Others People's Money" and "Barbarians at the Gate" you have an idea of what a takeover artist is all about. You have an understanding what they look for in a company: high cash flow. We are suggesting that you think in terms of High Cash Flow in analyzing a company and look at the cash flow patterns when searching for potential investments. Companies that are managing themselves on the principles of ongoing improvement are companies that are keenly interested in how much cash flow will be available to pay off the debts they have and re-invest in expanding their markets and retaining their current customers. Realize though that a company with a cash flow that does not change much from year to year makes an attractive takeover candidate. Takeover specialists are more interested in pre-tax (rather than after-tax) cash flow because interest on the debt created by the LBO will be tax deductible and taxes will be lower. Congress may change this, but now taxes are decreased by the interest on huge buyout costs.

Normally one might think cash flow would be earnings less capital expenditures, but in the world of TOC economics we must consider depreciation (and/or depletion), which must be added to that figure (because it was previously subtracted in determining earnings). You can get the data either from the company's income statement (usually easier), or its consolidated statement of cash flows, in the annual report. If you use the cash flow statement, look for the line that says "net cash provided by operating activities." Use either pre-tax or after-tax earnings, depending of which cash flow you wish to find. Then, divide that cash flow by the number of stockholder shares outstanding to get cash flow per share.

Cash Flow Per Share

Net profit plus non-cash charges such as depreciation (the accounting procedure which allocates the cost of a fixed asset over its useful life), depletion and amortization less preferred dividends, (a share of earnings paid to a stockholder by a corporation), all divided by the number of common shares outstanding (the number of common shares of stock outstanding at the end of the year, including stock held by the company in its treasury).

Why Cash Flow Equals Earnings Plus Depreciation.
It may seem strange to add depreciation as a "source" of funds. Aging of a building or other assets certainly does not generate cash. In TOC accounting we must remember that on the income statement, we started with gross income (from sales etc) and subtracted a depreciation expense (along with other expense items) to get net (taxable) income. It was a sort of "phantom" expense because it was not a cash-out-of-pocket expense, but it was nevertheless subtracted to get the correct before-tax earnings figure. Therefore, in real TOC accounting terms if the source of funds statement is to account for all the funds and we start the computation with net earnings from the income statement, we must add depreciation back again. Welcome to the world of cost accounting! But remember the cost accountants are only playing with the deck of cards given to them. Again, this highlights the difference between accounting, and economics and finance. We are attempting to gather accounting data to paint a picture of economics—TOC economics— in order to analyze various investment opportunities. We are more concerned about the pattern movement than the accounting calculation of inventory and depreciation accuracy presents. As stated earlier, we found no significant pattern movement if the TOC accounting calculation for depreciation was performed, or if the numbers were taken straight from the balance sheet the pattern was the same. The exact dollar number is different. The pattern is the key.

Return on Equity (ROE); Profit Growth and Return on Investment.
The number one question people ask financial planners about a stock is what percent return did it make on the money that investors put into it? The statement contains information in and of itself to answer the question. The percent return on stockholder's (investor, owners) equity is called "return on equity" ("ROE" for short). To calculate ROE, find the "Net Income" (usually the last item) on a company's income statement and divide it by stockholder's equity from the balance sheet (original equity plus retained earnings), and you will see a number. Hopefully that number is greater than the interest being paid on your checking ac-

count or passbook savings.

$$\textbf{Return On Equity} = \frac{\text{Net Income: \$300,000}}{\text{Stockholders Equity: \$800,000}} = 38\%*$$

*18% is industry norm

The example above shows a high return on equity; higher than other shares of other companies in the industry. This can be due to (1) a high return on assets or (2) high utilization of debt, or both (1) and (2).

$$\textbf{Profit Margin} = \frac{\text{Net Income: \$500,000}}{\text{Sales: \$2,500,000}} = 20\%*$$

*6% is industry norm

The profit margin pattern is a good indication that the company has its fingers on the pulse of cost control, and other OE pattern items.

Profit is what's left over after the costs of running a business are paid. Profit is the goal for business. Without it, there won't be a business for very long.

Profit Margin is the easiest way to tell how well management is controlling OE, when compared with other companies. Different industries exhibit different Profit Margin profiles. Very competitive industries, like grocery stores, tend to report low profit margins. Industries with high barriers to entry or high capital costs tend to display higher profit margins. An example might be an automobile manufacturer or steel manufacturers. Companies with dominant brands also tend to report higher profit margins. Examples would include GM, Pepsi, Oracle, Microsoft, and Coke.

Profit Margin is an integral part of Return On Equity (ROE). A higher profit margin usually implies a higher ROE.

If the company that you are monitoring owes very little debt, then it is reasonable to assume that the managers are earning high profit margins or turning assets effectively. This would be shown by a relatively high value for *Return On Assets*. You need to watch this as a trend in the pattern model.

If, on the other hand, the company is deeply in debt, then a high ROE is likely due to leverage. The *Return On Assets* value will bear this out. In this example, while ROE is high, ROA would be relatively low.

Return On Equity can also help you evaluate trends in a business. And ROE can also be used to compare the performance between companies in the same industry.

One word of caution when using Return On Equity from a TOC perspective. Financial statements show assets at their book value, which is the purchase price minus depreciation. They do not show replacement costs. Depreciation must be adjusted from the balance sheet to the OE side to truly see the TOC effects. A business with older assets should show higher rates of Return On Equity than a business with newer assets in normal reporting and trend analysis. Therefore, you will need to do a little checking into the companies to make the necessary adjustments in your thinking and analyzing as you view the data in the pattern graphs.

Return on Investment

$$\text{ROI} = \frac{\text{Net Income: } \$500,000}{\text{Total Investments \& Assets: } \$2,500,000} = 20\%*$$

*13% is industry norm

ROI yields between 0 to 10% are considered LOW. 11% to 20% are good and 21% to 30% are high. The return on investment & assets (TOC Inventory basically) shows that the company manages its TOC Inventory in a good productive manner and is doing better than the competitors in converting Inventory into throughput.

Return on Sales

Net After Tax Profit divided by Annual Net Sales, indicating the level of profit from each dollar of sales. This ratio can be used as a predictor of the company's ability to withstand changes in prices or market conditions. From a TOC perspective this is important when patterns are shifting in competitive situations, price wars or convergence.

Collection period in days

$$\text{Average collect period} = \frac{\text{Accounts Receivable: } \$400,000}{\text{Average Daily Sales: } \$10,000} = 40*$$

*35 is industry norm

The example here shows that the company does not collect its receivables (bills) as quickly as the industry average. A poor pattern in utilizing the assets at hand.

Inventory

This word as used by TOC accounting will be a new term for the more traditional investor. Inventory is more than Items such as raw materials, work-in-process and finished goods. It includes all equipment, property and like kind. Hence this needs to be pulled from a few different line items in most reports and grouped together with other items that will comprise the TOC category called Inventory. Inventory accounts for all unused parts and raw materials and finished but unsold products. It represents what accountants call "temporarily idle capital" — capital that at the moment is not earning any return on the money tied up in it.

Companies working on the premise of a process of ongoing improvement work hard to keep inventories low—trying all the time through their computer systems to keep just enough inventory to meet customer demands promptly, but no excess inventory sitting around on shelves in warehouses strategically placed off of major Interstate Highway exchanges! For that reason, it is interesting to look at "inventory turnover per year," which is Sales divided by year-end inventory. That is, how often annually does inventory get used and replaced? What you are looking for in inventory turnover and the ratio thereof is how efficiently management is managing the inventory in this company. Remember it is Inventory that gets converted to throughput and thus the ability to produce free cash flow.

$$\textbf{Inventory Turnover} = \frac{\text{Sales: } \$2,500,000}{\text{Year End Inventory: } \$500,000} = *5$$

*7 is industry norm

In our example the company is showing a pattern in their inventory turnover that is not desirable, meaning the company generates fewer sales per dollar of inventory that is sitting around and has less efficient inventory and cost control than its competitors. Inventory turnover is a measure of efficiency. General rule of thumb is the higher the number the better. The standard does differ by what industry the company is in and you must examine if the company is in a non-competitive market or is the inventory in this company is moving towards obsolescence. Not all low turnover is bad depending on the industry. Companies that specialize in very high priced items with high profits may not move their inventory often. What pattern does this indicate for a process of ongoing improvement?

Sales: Inventory

Another ratio you may want to consider building into your future models is the Sales to Inventory Ratio. Annual Net Sales divided by Inventory value. This gives a picture of how quickly inventory turns over. In the ratio we have developed we look at the actual inventory turns for the pattern we developed. Knowing how quickly inventory turns over relative to sales will tell you several key TOC components. What we are looking at here is Throughput velocity and inventory stocking issues. Ratios below the industry norm suggest high levels of inventory. High ratios could indicate product levels insufficient to satisfy demand in a timely manner. This has an effect on throughput patterns.

Sales to Employee Ratio

This is another key ratio. When it is hard to determine actual employee cost in the OE reporting numbers, or whether or not the company is adding more employees unnecessarily, you can use this ratio as a guide to see if patterns are developing. This ratio is usually a measure of efficiency. It will often tell you something about how the company has or has not implemented systems and technology to make the company more efficient. Or it could indicate that the talent and skills of the company and its people are high or low.

$$\text{Sales to Employee} = \frac{\text{Sales: } \$80,000,000}{\text{Number of Employees: } 600} = \$133,333$$

The higher the ratio numbers the better. The key to watch is if customer satisfaction is stable. If the pattern in sales is the same and the sales to employee ration is coming down, you need to look for patterns of why management is adding people versus looking at technology.

Dividend Payout

We must remember that a dividend payout is a share of earnings paid to a stockholder by a corporation. You need to monitor the pattern that develops for payouts. What pattern sign or movement is being expressed when dividend payouts are very large? When there are no dividend payouts for well-established companies over extended periods of time? Reinvestment of a proper amount of dividends helps the company to expand markets, retain customers and improve efficiencies.

$$\text{Dividend Payout} = \frac{\text{Dividend per Share: } \$0.15}{\text{EPS: } \$0.23} = 65\%*$$

*10% is industry norm

What does this mean for patterns recognition? The payout ratio means that this company is rewarding its investors more, but retaining fewer earnings for expanding markets, retaining customers and improving efficiencies. Is the company plowing more of its earnings back into the business for better management of ongoing improvement or is it paying dividends out very liberally? Ask the question what is going on with management. What pattern is developing?

Other Important Annual Report Items

Management's letter: This letter usually details management's intended direction for the company and its plans for the future. Be wary when the President or CFO uses terms like *challenging, shifting market conditions, we followed the advice of the analyst, industry analyst gave us inaccurate information, we are cutting costs again to bring cost in line, we are experiencing revenue reversals*. Management may be trying to mask a mediocre, flat quarter/year. You may want to check the prior year's reports to see if the company reached the goals that it had set earlier. We would suggest extending the model four or maybe eight extra quarters to take into account the previous year and what was said in relationship to what was accomplished. Did the company meet management's projections? Are its acquisitions decreasing costs and improving earnings? This will have an effect on the patterns and models you build.

Did the letter mention concerns that the company has been experiencing? Did it explain why failures or near misses happened, or say how they were going to correct problems? Are management's goals and objectives solid ones that are attainable and for the greater good of the company as a whole and not just for the good of the managers, or selected departments; will management be rewarded for the attainment of the goal? Does the report contain abstract language like "making the suppliers feel good"?

Is the company investing in new plants and equipment or is it closing plants? New plants or capacity can be a good sign of increase in throughput that business is increasing and markets are growing while retaining customers. Conversely, new plants could mean that management is foolishly building capacity it does not need. New plants cost a lot of money and depress earnings in the short term, but usually reduce costs in the long run. The key here is to work the model to fully visualize if Throughput (T) is increasing, and Operating Expense (OE) and Inventory (I) are decreasing or remaining flat.

Auditor's statement: In publicly traded companies the accounting firm will use what is called GAAP, generally accepted accounting principles in preparing the financial statements. If the last paragraph uses words like "except for" and "subject to" it may mean that there are discrepancies. Such exceptions are rare, say 1 out of 100 companies, but if you see these exceptions in the auditor's statement, beware! A future problem or write-off may be in the wings. The company may have "twisted the arm" of the accounting firm not to publish the exceptions.

Footnotes: This section will contain some of the most valuable information in the report. Footnotes are like the "fine print" on the used car purchase statement. Footnotes are often the "worth the price of admission." Items having major impacts, like outstanding lawsuits, changes in accounting practices, taxes owed and management stock options may be covered only in footnotes. These items will have impact in your model going forward. They can and will add to the OE equations and sometimes will drive down throughput because management and others are distracted especially in lawsuits. Watch for companies that change their accounting practices, such as changes in inventory valuation (last in first out, LIFO, to first in first out, FIFO, or vice versa). A firm that changes these practices every couple of years may be trying to "dress up" the income statement, to make throughput look better than it actually is. They may change an accounting policy to make a poor year look better. This is where the pattern models will assist you in catching this change. LIFO is generally a more conservative method that values inventory more accurately during inflation periods. The majority of American firms use LIFO.

Look also for pension fund liabilities. Management may reduce a firm's pension plan contributions by raising the projected rate of return on its pension investments. Higher projected returns suggest the company pension fund will grow faster. That allows the company to reduce the amount of money it puts into the pension plan for that year. This "newly realized" money falsely reflects increased profits. You will need to compensate for this in the model.

Management may use this tactic to turn a poor or money-losing year into a fair year. And for some a fair year may mean they receive a bonus whereas in a poor year they do not.

In conclusion, the words of Lewis Richardson, the "father of modern meteorology, seem appropriate for pattern movements:

"Big whorls have little whorls
Which feed on their velocity,
And little whorls have lesser whorls
And so on to viscosity."

CHAPTER FIVE
Using the Roadmap Model

"Let's work the problem people. Let's not make things worse by guessing."

—Gene Krantz in Apollo 13

We have been stressing all through this book that our roadmap model is not a radical departure, as much as a logical extension of the great work already done in stock analysis. Nevertheless, we also believe the approach offers a different perspective, which we have attempted to explain in the prior three chapters. This chapter focuses on an explanation of the roadmap model, conceptually how it works, where to find the data, formulas to use, and so forth. In the appendix you will find a section on functional use of the roadmap model. The intent here is to help the reader assimilate accurate results and help him draw appropriate conclusions. The roadmap model is not a plug and play magic formula, and it could be costly to use it in such a fashion. The roadmap model is meant to be an aid to the TOC Thinking Processes described in this book. Indeed, we have selected companies that we hoped would offer differing situations from different industries, but might illustrate how the same phenomena in two companies might be interpreted very differently because of the larger context surrounding each company, such that, one might make a decision to buy one company and reject the other.

Where To Begin

Working the models with the digital spreadsheet.

Source of the Data

We have found the best source data is in Annual Reports or Quarterly Reports (10-Q) in either the company website, or the Edgar database provided by the SEC (http://www.sec.gov/cgi-bin/srch-edgar). Most 10-Qs are in text or HTML format. Most Annual Reports are in Adobe Acrobat. Many of these same annual reports and 10-Qs are in public libraries, University libraries and they will all be mailed to you if you request them from the company. After all, this is the data that the company themselves give to regulators that say, "to the best of our knowledge this is an accurate reflection of our financial status."

In addition, you will need some data not found in the Annual and Quarterly reports, specifically number of employees and stock price data for the past two years. The best source of employee data is Standard and Poor's.

For historic stock price information, there is a wonderful area on Yahoo (http://chart.yahoo.com/d), which will provide stock prices on a daily weekly or monthly basis all adjusted for stock splits.
Be sure to look at MorningStar (http:// www. Morning star.com/), MSN Money (moneycentral.msn.com/investor/),
The Street (www.street.com), and for a variety of links and tools go to Super Investor (www.superstarinvestor.com/dirlinks.html).
There are many others on the web today and most libraries also have sources of information, such as Value Line and others where you can obtain the information you may need to build your own models.

Our suggestion is when working with an on-line data source, library source material or the company website, you should stay with that one source for your total company analysis, especially if you are just beginning to learn the method and process. As you become more comfortable and experienced in the nuances of the various on-line sites and home pages of corporations, you can begin to experiment with mix and matching data sources. You will find that not all sources report data exactly the same in all circumstances. The data may be called the same in some situations but analyzed and reported differently. Do not become alarmed with this; it is perfectly normal and common in the world of investing.

We also strongly recommend that you keep a "notes" section either in your spreadsheet or a word processing document, or in a separate notebook to record any adjustments or nuances you may have made to the data before entering it into the model. We also suggest you keep a simple calculator close at hand, or use an online calculator that can perform simple addition, subtraction, percentage, division and multiplication calculations. When working with the data electronically, have both a browser open for the data in HTML and text format and an Acrobat reader open for the data in Adobe format, as most companies will provide data and especially annual reports in Acrobat formats. Keep in mind if you are not accustomed to using Acrobat, you cannot cut and paste data from an Acrobat file. You will need to either remember the data or write it down before entering it into the model. Try to keep them in chronological order from oldest to most current so you can easily move back and forth between time periods. You will need access to all this data if you are to complete the spreadsheet in a timely manner.

Time Period

The first decision the reader must make is what time period he wants to analyze. The spreadsheet provides eight time periods, which could be 8 quarters, or eight years. Additionally, the spreadsheet file is not locked, so the reader could expand it if so desired. Most of our research was done using the most recent 8 quarters, as that data is the most current and therefore the most telling as to where the company is now and where they are heading. Remember, we are looking for pattern recognition.

Important: when moving between Quarterly and Annual Reports some arithmetic is necessary. In order to derive certain fourth quarter data, primarily the data from the Income Statement, you may have to subtract the preceding three quarters (normally provided in a summary column on the third Quarterly Report, entitled "Nine Months Ending") from the annual data found in the annual report. For example, to derive fourth quarter sales you may have to subtract the nine months sales, ending Sept 30, from the annual sales found in the December Annual Report. And so on.

Throughput Items

The first tab of the model's spreadsheet is the Throughput Items. These are the Total Sales, Sales Growth, Profit Growth and Profit Margin. Remember we discussed the need to make the necessary TOC- centric adjustments before entering data into the spreadsheet. We have discovered in many sample models that in certain situations and companies if the adjustments are not made there may not be "material" differences in the results shown in the pattern graphs. These numbers are the basic data to determine what sales and profits are, if they are growing or declining, and at what velocity (very important!). They are quite easy to identify. Total Sales will come right off the top line (or top category if they are sub items) of the Income Statement for the quarter or year required. It will be described as Sales or Revenue in most cases. Sales growth is simply the difference in Sales from time period to time period (so you will need the financial report of one period before the 8 periods you are analyzing). It will be the same for Profit Growth; it is the difference from one period to the next. You will find Profits almost always listed as Net Income on the Income Statement. We always used the Net-Net Income after all expenses—after taxes and depreciation and everything else is taken out. Finally, Profit Margin = Net Income/Total Sales.

Enter the data into the spreadsheet cell. Enter each quarter with its corresponding data point from the source data you are using.

Throughput Patterns

Throughput Ratios include Sales Per Employee, Profit per Employee, Expenses as a Percent of Sales, Research & Development as a Percent of Sales and Collection Period in days. These ratios will help provide an idea of how operationally efficient the company is in driving its throughput, and if it is an area of improvement, or one that is being ignored. Sales per Employee are simply the Total Sales for the period divided by the number of employees during that time period. Finding employee data by quarter is difficult, therefore you must be aware of any major shifts in personnel and, in such cases, you may have to do some estimating. Similarly, Profits Per Employee is Net Income divided by the number of employees. Expenses as a Percent of Sales is all the expenses involved in running the business divided by total sales, or revenue, for the period. Expenses are found on the Income Statement, and include such things as Cost of Sales, Operating, Selling and General Administrative, Interest Costs and so forth, but not Taxes. Collection Period is simply the Accounts Receivable, found on the Balance Sheet under Assets divided by Sales per Day or Sales divided by 360 (days). If it is quarterly data divide by 90. (Receivables/(Sales/90)).

Enter the data into the spreadsheet cell. Enter each quarter with its corresponding data point from the source data you are using.

Inventory Items

Inventory Items include Property, Plant & Equipment, Balance Sheet Number, Inventory Turnover Ratio, Return on Equity and Return on Assets. These numbers assist in your understanding of how efficiently the company is managing the process of turning raw material into finished goods, how resource intensive the company is, what kind of returns on its investment the company is getting (and if they are increasing and at what velocity) and whether it is an area of improvement for the company. Property, Plant & Equipment is found under Assets on the Balance Sheet. The Balance Sheet Number is a calculation and one that requires some judgment in many cases. The Balance Sheet Number focuses on Assets. The objective is to measure all the assets the company uses to conduct its operations. It includes all Current Assets: Cash, Receivables, Inventories and so forth. It also included long-term assets such as Property, Plant & Equipment, and Capital Leases and so forth, minus any depreciation. (A good rule of thumb for the Balance Sheet Number = Current Assets + Long Term Assets − Depreciation.) Inventory Ratio = Sales/Inventory. Return on Equity will be equal to the Net Income/Shareholder Equity (found on the Balance Sheet) and Return on Assets = Net Income/Total Assets.

Enter the data into the spreadsheet cell. Enter each quarter with its corresponding data point from the source data you are using.

Inventory Patterns

Inventory Ratios include Ratio of Debt to Equity, Ratio of Long Term Debt to Equity and Interest Expense as a Percent of Sales. These numbers will give the reader an idea of how well the company is using leverage; whether debt is increasing and how expensive debt is for the company. The Ratio of Debt to Equity is calculated by dividing Total Debt, that is the Short and Long Term Debt found in the liabilities side of the Balance Sheet. (Long term Debt includes any obligation, which is not listed under Short term Debt or Shareholder Equity. Such items as Deferred Taxes are Long Term Debts.) Ratio of Long Term Debt to equity equals Long Term Debt/Shareholder Equity. Interest Expense As a Percent of Sales will equal Interest taken from the Expense section of the Income Statement divided by Total Sales.

Enter the data into the spreadsheet cell. Enter each quarter with its corresponding data point from the source data you are using.

Goal Ratios

Goal ratios include High Stock Price to Earnings Per Share, Low Stock Price to Earnings Per Share, Average Stock Price to Earnings Per Share, Free Cash Flow Per Share, Free Cash Flow, Return on Sales and Dividend Payout Ratio. These Ratios tell us how well the company is meeting its goals of making money, rewarding the shareholders and how much real cash the company is generating to put back into the business. Getting historical stock price information and dividing it by the Earnings Per Share can calculate the first three measures. They are, in effect, three different snapshots of the Price/Earnings Ratio, which attempts to tell us how expensive a stock is for each dollar of earnings a company realizes. (The EPS data is usually found at the bottom of the Income Statement. Otherwise you can calculate EPS by dividing Net Income by the total outstanding number of shares.) Free Cash Flow is the amount of real cash generated by the business. A good estimate of Free Cash Flow is found on the Cash Flow Statement. Operating Activities, or something along those lines, will describe it as Cash Flows From Operating Activities or Net Cash Provided. This number will be used for both the Free Cash Flow entry, and divided by the Number of Outstanding Shares will be the entry for

Free Cash Flow per Share. Getting the correct number of outstanding shares can be problematic. Once again, Standard and Poor's may be the best resource for that data. Return on Sales is simply the net income divided by Total Sales. Dividend Payout Ratio is the declared dividend per share usually found at the bottom of the Income Statement.

Enter the data into the spreadsheet cell. Enter each quarter with its corresponding data point from the source data you are using. Once you have successfully entered all these data points, you can begin assessing the merits of the company. You will notice that as soon as the data points are entered into the cells, the corresponding graph for the pattern recognition appears. You have now produced the pattern movement.

You will be looking for Patterns of Increases in Throughput and decreases in Operating Expense and Investment or justified increases based on the consistency and velocity of the Throughput increases. You will then need to verify your conclusions with a qualitative view of the company. What is their go to market strategy? What changes are they making in managing their Supply Chain? What is the makeup of the management team? What news is available about this company? What is happening with their competitors? What is the macro environment (their industry, the general economy) like?

Finally, if the company looks attractive, you have one more key decision to make. At what price is the company attractive? Is the company expensive or cheap? The P/E ratio is one such measure and it should be looked at as a measure of the price of earnings. However, as mentioned above, the search for a measure of the intrinsic value of a company has led some of the greatest minds on investing to create many different algorithms. We offer a TOC-based algorithm here. The formula is simple and measures the key variable of the Roadmap model against the risk free rate of return in order to create a relative measure of intrinsic value. The formula is Target Stock Price = Free Cash Flow Per Share/Long Term Treasury Rate. The Treasury Rate can be either the 10 or 30 year Treasury Rate. We use the ten year since the thirty year bond is going away and the ten year rate is a better time frame with which to evaluate a buy and hold strategy, given how fast companies rise and fall today. So if Free Cash Flow per Share = 5 and the ten year Treasury was yielding 5%, then the Target price = 5/.05 = $100. In this example, the stock is an attractive buy under $100.

In the next section, we will look at some case studies to see how this all comes together. In the appendix, you will find instructions on how to load the model.

CHAPTER SIX
Case Studies of Publicly Traded Companies

Wal-Mart
Ready to break out?

Our analysis of Wal-Mart covers the period 2000-2001. In that time the company has traded in a semi-tight range between roughly $50-$60/share. Which means if you have been lucky enough to buy it whenever it hit $50 and sell it whenever it hit $60 you'd be making a 20% profit. Would the Roadmap tool have helped you call such short term moves? Absolutely not. We want to state emphatically that if you are looking for a trading pattern for short-term stock moves, you are in the wrong place. If you are accumulating Wal-Mart shares, or thinking about doing so, your average price is probably in the $53-$54 range which means you might have a few dollars of profit. Is a strategy of accumulating shares in Wal-Mart a good investment? Will it yield a return worthy of the risks?

Wal-Mart is a popular investment because they do so many things so well. They are masters in the area of distribution, logistical planning of their stores, operational efficiency, and vendor management, competitive pricing and so forth. And given the uncertain economy of 2002, they attract shoppers who are on a limited budget. The biggest risk to their continued growth is probably whether or not they have saturated their market. Are there geographic areas still to develop, which can fuel growth? Are we in a deflationary cycle, which will continue to depress prices?

The data in the tool shows some very interesting patterns. Insert your CD into your computer and load the excel spreadsheet called Wal-Mart so you can examine the charts we are discussing. First, the Throughput Items (see chart) show a company whose sales are trending upwards nicely, if cyclically. However, profit margin is erratic at best. The second sheet, Throughput Patterns, shows flatter Sales per Employee, and Profit per Employee increasing strongly, and slightly increasing expenses. Looking at the Inventory Items, this reveals a growing asset base and increasing Operational Assets (Balance Sheet Number). Inventory turn has stayed relatively constant while Return on Equity has remained strong, although Return on Assets has been up and down. The Inventory Patterns reflect Wal-Mart's strong debt management as those ratios are decreasing.

The first three columns in the Goal Patterns sheet are different views of Price Earnings ratios based on the high, low and average stock prices. You can see that the stock price to earnings is trending down, meaning earnings are getting more inexpensive. P/E's are a relative measure. They only really make sense in relation to other companies in the same industry and the markets as a whole. While they are a useful measure, P/E's, or the earnings multiples as they are also called, are not etched in stone. They are dependent on the quality of reported earnings, which we are all now painfully aware can be suspect, and the time frame. Are these current earnings or future projected earnings? The Free Cash Flow Per Share and Free Cash Flow columns offer another view of the financial strength of the company. In Wal-Mart's case the story is not overly attractive. The Free Cash Flow numbers are erratic if you compare the corresponding quarters for each year (Q1 2000 to Q1 2001 and so on) you will see Free Cash Flow up in one comparison and down the next. The pattern is unclear.

The overall outlook on Wal-Mart is neutral. Gross Throughput appears to be increasing but asset growth is outpacing Throughput, which would account for the eroding profit margins. In TOC terms, Throughput is rising, Operational Expense is falling but Investment is rising. This conclusion is supported by the flat employee to sales ratio (they are adding employees), and even though debt ratios are declining somewhat, the eroding free cash numbers tell us they are burning cash. Wal-Mart focuses on operational efficiency, and that efficiency is being undermined by the increase in assets. Finally, applying the intrinsic value formula to the estimated current cash flow/share would put a target price on Wal-Mart of $41-$42/share. If we use all of 2001 to measure free cash flow to account for cyclical changes (which would be Free Cash Flow from Q1 +Q2 +Q3 +Q4)/Number of outstanding shares/Treasury Bond = $47. Currently, Wal-Mart is trading in the low $50's. Wal-Mart is a great retailer and would not be a bad stock to own if the price was right.

UnitedHealth Group
Are there any legs left?

UnitedHealth Group provides both managed healthcare services, as well as unbundled healthcare management products and services. United has organized itself into several business units in order to better understand the diverse healthcare markets they serve and provide better quality to each. The business units include: United Healthcare, which provides health care coverage and services to employers and consumers; Ovations, which offers health programs and services targeted to people age 50 and over; Uniprise, which offers customized health solutions to the Fortune 500; Specialized Care Services, a unit that offers specialized services through subsidiary companies; Ingenix, which offers worldwide drug development and marketing services to the pharmaceutical industry; and research and data and consulting services to insurance companies, health care providers, private corporations and governments; and UnitedHealth Capital, which offers capital for startup health care companies. Obviously, UnitedHealth Group is far more than just another health coverage company. As the United States continues to age, such companies should be appealing to investors looking for areas of consistent growth.

Our analysis of UnitedHealth Group covers the period 2000-2001. In the years analyzed, the company's shares have seen a remarkable run from $26/share to $70/share. It has been one of the rare shining lights in the midst of a very tough bear market. The obvious questions on the investor's mind have to be: if I own the shares, do I continue to hold them or add to my position? Should I take profits here? If I don't own UnitedHealth, does it still make sense to buy? Will it yield a return worthy of the risks?

The data in the tool should help answer these questions. First the **Throughput Items** show a company with continued rising Sales, up 16% in the 8 quarters. Profits, however, have begun to flatten out. The second sheet, **Throughput Items**, shows Sales per Employee and Profit per Employee continue to rise while expenses remain steady. The **Inventory Items** sheet reveals steady increase in investment in Property, Plant and Equipment and Operational Assets (Balance Sheet Number) with gains in Return on Equity and Assets beginning to flatten out. The **Inventory Patterns** show rises in the debt structure at United that could be a cause for concern. The question is, why are debts increasing relative to equity?

In **Goal Patterns**, the three Price to EPS columns show a rising trend reflecting that earnings are much more expensive than they were two years ago. The Free Cash Flow columns show a much more uneven view of the financial strength of the company. Free Cash Flow fell but recovered nicely before flattening out in the last two quarters. On a per share basis, Free Cash Flow has remained flat.

It appears that the stock price run up of the last two years is at best going to be on hold. Gross Throughput continues to increase while profit margins have flattened; fixed assets have grown, as has long-term debt. The company looks to have made some large investments, which may or may not have positioned it well for further long-term growth. The situation needs to be researched. The intrinsic value formula to the estimated current cash flow/share would put a target price on United of $70/share. It seems fair to say that at $90/share United is a bit overvalued. UnitedHealth is a company doing many things very well. At the right price it looks like a great way to play the health provider industry. At the right price.

Ethan Allen Interiors, Inc
The beginning of a new trend?

Ethan Allen Interiors manufactures a full range of home furnishing products and accessories. They also operate over 300 retail stores throughout the United States Although they have always been known for high quality products, Ethan Allen is looking to broaden out and reach more consumers. Ethan Allen's strategy is centered around several key objectives: growth through addition of new stores, relocating and renovating existing stores, upgrading personnel, improving warehouse process, introducing product innovations such as Horizons by Ethan Allen and EA Elements, developing marketing programs that create a message of style and accessibility to consumers, strengthening the Ethan Allen brand, and leveraging the Internet.

Our analysis of Ethan Allen covers the period 2000-2001. In the years analyzed, the company's shares have trended nicely upwards from $23/share to $41/share. The question for potential investors in this company: is Ethan Allen well positioned for long-term growth?

The data in the tool should help answer these questions. First the **Throughput Items** show a company with erratic Sales and Profits, and profit margin has steadily declined. However, the second sheet, **Throughput Patterns**, shows Sales per Employee and expenses have all remained fairly steady, while Profits and ROI have declined and then rebounded. The **Inventory Items** sheet, shows a slight rise in Property, Plant and Equipment while Inventory Turnover has held even. Returns on Equity and Assets have fallen but recently rebounded. The **Inventory Patterns** show large reductions in the debt structure and interest expense.

In the **Goal Patterns**, the three Price to EPS columns show a rising trend reflecting that earnings are much more expensive than they were two years ago. The Free Cash Flow columns show that Free Cash Flow has been declining until that last two quarters when it rebounded. One could conclude that Ethan Allen has come through the bear market in relatively good shape and is beginning to see a positive business environment again.

If the last two quarters are the beginning of a new pattern, then Ethan Allen may be an attractive stock. Gross Throughput and Profit have reversed their downward slide, and they have managed inventory well and brought down long-term debt significantly. A qualitative assessment needs to be carried out to determine how well the company is executing on strategy, and managing its supply chain. The intrinsic value formula to the estimated current cash flow/share would put a target price on Ethan Allan of $44/share. As of this writing it is trading at $38/share. Ethan Allen may be a good example of a solid long-term play. If they continue to expand throughput and manage short and long-term expenses as they have in the recent past, the share price will appreciate nicely.

Philip Morris (Altria)
"It's not hard to get along with somebody else's troubles."
—Steve Goodman

Philip Morris, a producer of tobacco, foods and beverages, has long been respected as one of the best-managed companies in the world. It has also been one of the most controversial. Anti tobacco lobby groups see Philip Morris as the enemy, attacking either its tobacco or its processed foods division, Kraft Foods. Anti-alcohol lobbyists will have to take their fight elsewhere as the company has just sold its Miller Beer operation for $5 Billion. The company has also garnered a reputation for excellence in management, corporate strategy, career pathing and human resource management and philanthropic support. Philip Morris donates large sums of money to a variety of causes, including hunger, domestic violence and the arts. However, despite its reputation as one of the best-managed companies in the US, the price of its shares spiraled downward. The commonly understood explanation was the decline was has happening because of concern over pending tobacco related lawsuits.

We looked at the years 2000-2001. In the years analyzed, the company's shares have rebounded back to its recent range, moving from $23/share to $50/share. It has been one of the better investments in this bear market. Although the share price has returned to normal levels, there are several key questions about Philip Morris, as the company seems to be in state where their strategy may be changing. The company is in the process of spinning off or selling a few business units. This year a portion of Kraft was spun off as a separate IPO, and as mentioned above, Miller was recently sold. What is its long-term strategy? Will the high quality of management continue? What is their exposure to future lawsuits? How will they evolve their business over time?

The data in the tool is very interesting in regard to this company. First the **Throughput Items** show a company with erratic Sales and Profit Growth. Profit Margin bounced around between 9.5 and 11.5. In the second sheet, **Throughput Patterns**, Sales per Employee, Profit per Employee and ROI show the same up and down pattern while expenses have remained fairly steady. The **Inventory Items** sheet shows everything holding steady except for a significant jump in Property, Plant and Equipment. The **Inventory Patterns** show a jump in the debt and expense structure that was as quickly reversed.

In the **Goal Patterns**, the three Price to EPS columns show a stock with very inexpensive earnings returning to more normal levels. The Free Cash Flow columns show that free cash Flow has been very erratic although they did enjoy a nice rise corresponding to the reversal of the debt and expense issue in the same quarters.

It appears that Big MO's problems were not all in the courtroom. The data portrays very uneven performance in the last 8 quarters with no discernible pattern. Yes they legal headlines drove the price artificially low, and as that pressure subsided the stock returned to its former level and has stagnated. The company appears to be going through major changes in its strategy and product mix, including a name change of the company to the Altria Group. This rough sailing could be the beginning of a well-defined new direction or reflective of a large corporation in serious churn. The intrinsic value formula to the estimated current cash flow/share would put a target price on Philip Morris of $96/share. As of this writing it is trading at $56/share, indicating a lot of upside potential. Given the historic track record of solid management execution, Big MO may be a big play.

Cemex
Is this a real TOC Company?

Cemex (cemex.com) Is a leading worldwide producer and marketer of cement and ready-mix products to both individual homebuilders and to large industrial contractors. In the years analyzed, the company's shares have rebounded back to its recent range, moving from $20/share to $30/share. Our analysis of Cemex covers the period 2000-2001. To begin, we need to first understand who Cemex is and what they do. They are a cement company, now one of the three largest in the world. They have their own operations in thirty countries, but trade with over sixty countries. According to their latest statistics, they have seventy-seven million metric tons of production capacity. It is easy to see why a company of such a large scale would need an efficient production management strategy. Their operations are primarily based in Mexico, Spain, Venezuela, Costa Rica, The Philippines, Panama, The Dominican Republic, Egypt, Columbia, and the southwest United States. Cement is a unique product and needs to be handled differently, especially in matters of logistics, than most other products. On-time delivery is key to their business, as the life of ready mix cement is relatively small. Cemex started using principles based on TOC techniques around 1996. At this time delivery of their product was promised to customers within a span of 3 hours of scheduled delivery time. Management knew that this was not going to continue to be acceptable from customers.

Cemex is very serious about customer service. They constantly strive to find new and better ways to serve their customers, to expand their markets, retain their customers and improve their efficiencies in a business that has extreme variables. Cemex uses technology in enabling the value chain to bring about zero latency and a real time enterprise. Because of the relatively small number of cement suppliers, Cemex understands the importance of customer loyalty. "In Egypt, approximately 95% of the company's cement is sold in bags throughout local distributors." Instances such as this, stress the importance of a system that can handle large commercial orders, and also cater to the needs of their smaller, loyal retail customers that many times are not in areas that are consider technologically enabled.

The data in the tool all point to the same question: what happened two quarters ago? First the **Throughput Items** show Sales and Profit Growth growing nicely until quarter seven. Then the bottom drops out. This pattern is reflected through almost all the other data. Profit Margin held steady until the same quarter, but rebounded nicely in quarter 8. In the second sheet, **Throughput Patterns**, Sales per Employee and Profit per Employee show the same pattern while expenses have remained fairly steady. The **Inventory Items** sheet shows fairly steady growth in assets, and consistency in return on equity and assets, although ROA shows the same big drop in Q7. The **Inventory Patterns** show the company kept debt and expense structure level.

In the **Goal Patterns**, the three Price to EPS columns show a declining ratio reflecting that earnings are less expensive (except for Q7). The Free Cash Flow columns show that free cash Flow has been growing moderately.

Cemex appears to be a company that is growing throughput and managing that growth well, except for the one bad quarter. The intrinsic value formula to the estimated current cash flow/share would put a target price on Cemex of $5/share. As of this writing it is trading at $30/share. Cemex, in its reporting, appears to understand the importance of managing according to TOC concepts. However, the stock is trading at a huge premium to a Cash Flow per share analysis. Additionally, the reason for the Q7 aberration needs to be understood. Cemex needs to execute its strategy if it is to have good long-term prospects.

General Electric
The house that Jack built

This is an illustration of two basic concepts. The first is that the tool can be used over different spans of time. In this analysis we used yearly increments rather than quarterly to get a longer term feel for a company. Even though the data from the earlier years is out of date, it does provide an interesting context. Second, we wanted to test how well the tool would have predicted stock price moves over a longer term. We chose GE because most people are well aware of the years of success Jack Welch had in building this giant. General Electric Company is a broadly diversified industrial corporation that is in the business of creating, manufacturing and marketing electrical products. GE had twelve business units that produce major household appliances, lighting products, industrial automation products, medical equipment, motors, electrical equipment, locomotives, power generator products, nuclear power products and airplane engines. GE also offers services that support many of their product lines. In addition, GE owns NBC, which offers broadcast services. Under Welch's leadership, GE has become known as one of the standards of excellence in corporate management, quality improvements, and financial prudence. In the last decade, Welch has become the most visible leader in corporate America, with his books and appearances on television.

Our analysis of General Electric covers the period 1994-2001. The data in the tool reveal much of what you would expect: seven years of consistently success and a correction in the eighth year, 2001. The **Throughput Items** show Sales and Profit Growth showing significant gains year after year until 2001, although Profit Margin increased and held its gains in 2001. In the second sheet, **Throughput Patterns**, Sales per Employee and Profit per Employee show the same pattern of increases, while expenses and Return on Investment have remained fairly steady. The **Inventory Items** sheets reflect the same strong growth in assets, maintenance of Inventory Turnover and Return on Equity and Assets, although it should be pointed out that the Inventory and ROE/ROA is maintained on a broadly increasing asset base, no small feat. The **Inventory Patterns** show that debt has increased, although long term debt has stayed almost even, again on a much bigger asset base 8 years later. Interest expense structure has stayed relatively flat. When viewing the Inventory or doing your own analysis of a company such as General Electric, consideration must be given to the balance sheet issues that reflect the diversification of financial services that represent GE Capital such as mortgage lending, banking, venture capital, equipment financing, credit card financing, mezzanine financing, long term investment, and so forth. Understanding that in finance when compiling TOC patterns consideration should be given to interest expense and interest income issues and what is considered assets is not always a tangible asset like you would have in a manufacturing or retail focused enterprise. Keep in mind GE spans the spectrum of industries that are represented on the balance sheet.

In the **Goal Patterns**, the three Price to EPS columns reflect the growth GE experienced but the multiples did not grow wildly in relation to the tremendous growth of the company. Free Cash Flow/share has grown steadily with the exception of 1997. Free Cash Flow shows the same pattern.

Except for the one dip in free cash flow growth, the tool was consistent in identifying a company with a consistently expanding throughput and free cash flow story. The patterns discovered here would have identified GE as a long term accumulate and hold company. GE's share price in 1994 started at $8.75 and rose steadily to $46.97 by end of year 2000. Our intrinsic value formula would have valued GE around $13-$14 in 1994, and even with the recent sell off to the $31-$33, our formula would value GE in the low $40's. The tool is not nimble enough to catch the short-term variations, nor is it designed to be. However, as illustrated in the GE example, it performs very well in identifying companies with superior long-term appreciation potential.

APPENDIX
Installing and Using the TOC Pattern Software Templates

Pattern Templates is a tool that will help you build your forecast investment analysis models, quickly and easily. It is a software template that runs on either IBM compatible or Macintosh computers. You will need a spreadsheet software program called Excel, sold by Microsoft. If you know the basics about Excel, it is simple to use. This model is offered on the CD in both Excel 2000 and Excel version 4.0 for those with older versions, and you can easily save it to newer versions or convert the templates to other products that perform spreadsheet functions. This section is a brief introduction to the features you will use most often while using the book to understand the various companies you may be analyzing.

This section assumes that you are familiar with the very basics of your computer. You should know, for example, how to use a mouse and how to work with your operating system whether that be Windows, OS/X, Linux and so forth. The instructions herein are based on the average user working in a Windows 95/98/2000 environment. If you feel you need help in these areas, refer to the documentation that came with your computer.

- Insert the CD (printed side up) into your CD-ROM drive.
- Choose EXCEL from the program section of your computer and open EXCEL. When EXCEL opens, go to FILE in the upper left hand corner and open. Choose OPEN and a dialogue box will appear. In the "look in" bar at the very top, open the selections to your CD drive, highlight it, and click. You will see various template files. Highlight the Pattern Template file and double click on the file to bring the template into the spreadsheet application.

The model that appears on your screen is a Pattern Template. It is a real, working model of the analysis we are describing in the book. None of the templates are locked so you have the option to customize them as you see fit. All you have to do is make a few of the changes that will customize Pattern Templates to become a model of your particular investment analysis. Pattern Template is complete and may be printed out immediately for you to review and analyze.

Pattern Templates is constructed in TABS, each of which has a special purpose and meaning. Each TAB is located at the bottom of the spreadsheet: They are labeled: Throughput Items; Throughput Patterns; Inventory Items; Inventory Patterns; Goal Patterns.

- The first TAB, called Inventory Items, is the section for you to type the important key data, which is found in your financial reports as we discuss in Chapter 5 *The Roadmap Model*. You will notice there are 4 columns called: Total Sales; Sales Growth; Profit Growth and Profit Margin. You will also notice there is a column called Quarters, which you use to place the appropriate source of information you are analyzing. If you wish you may substitute Quarters for Years. In any case you are looking at an 8-quarter pattern or 8 year pattern.

- Enter the date that corresponds to Total Sales of the quarter or year of the company you are analyzing. Type in the date or some other way for you to identify the quarter or year in the column and row that corresponds to the first quarter or first year you are analyzing.

- Now tab over to the right and the highlighted box should now be in the column and row that corresponds to the Total Sales box. Enter the total sales from the report you are using for the quarter or year you are analyzing in this box.

- Now tab over to the right and the highlighted box should now be in the column and row that corresponds to the Total Sales Growth box. Enter the total sales growth figure from the report you are using for the quarter or year you are analyzing in this box.

- Repeat this process for each box in each row and column for all eight quarters or years.

- You will notice as you enter the data into the row and column, the pattern graph automatically starts to build your pattern trend indicator models.

- When you have entered all the data into the necessary rows and columns you will see the graphs completely filled out and indicating a pattern.

- In the TABS marked "Items" and the TAB marked "Goal Patterns" you will notice two graphs. We separated out one graph to represent the one item that represents the "mother lode" of TOC Pattern movement.

Repeat the data entry process for each TAB in the spreadsheet model.

When you have finished building your model, go to the file section at the upper left hand corner of the spreadsheet and click it on. The drop down menu will appear. Choose the line called "Save as..."; as you click it, a dialogue box will appear. Enter in the bar at the very top the location you wish to save the file. Then in the bottom bar, choose the name you wish to call the file, and save it.

Our suggestion after you have completed a model is to print the graphs out. You need to print the graphs out Tab by Tab. After you print the graphs, look and compare the Throughput pattern trends with the Goal Pattern Trends. Then compare each with the Inventory trends. Remember you are looking for pattern movement that says throughput is rising and operating expenses/inventory are either constant or decreasing. Certain line items, as we discussed in the various chapters of the book, will indicate different trends and meaning to what is going on in the company, the industry or marketplace. All of these line items need to be taken into consideration when analyzing a company. But we all know that Cash is King so always check the Goal Pattern graphs to see if the company is truly growing from good to great over time. Realize that dips in Cash can mean the company made investments. You need to do some homework to gain your comfort levels. But the graph and patterns are giving you the warning signs.

These Pattern Templates will move along faster as you develop your style for organizing and searching for the data. Your first model will take you much longer that you expect because you are getting used to the placement and structure of the model and human nature will be dictating that you check and double check the data point to make sure you have placed the correct data in the appropriate cell in the spreadsheet. If you place any quarter or year out of sequence and that year has movement up or down the graph will show the anomaly in the pattern and you can go back and double check your data entry items. And most important, it will enable you to immediately begin testing the assumptions of your analysis.

HOW Pattern Templates WORKS

Pattern Templates begins with the changes you make to the cells (input) and then recalculates them into the graphs for a pattern view. Please reference Chapter 3 for the meaning behind the rows and columns in each of the Tabs. In the Goal Pattern Tab, the cash flow graphs should be most telling when compared to the Throughput Items and Throughput Pattern tabs. If you begin to see the proverbial roller coaster effect in the patterns you need to ask yourself first: is my data that I entered correct? Did I enter the data in the correct sequence? And then, if the answer is YES, to both of those questions, you should realize that you have just been given a "signal" to possible shifting patterns, or a sign of some issues in the company or in the industry or marketplace. In any case this becomes an indicator for you to look deeper and closer to the cause/effect in the roller coaster pattern.

Input drives output. The cells linking the input to the output graphs can be changed if you desire. And you can add or subtract lines or re-label them as you would in any spreadsheet model.
As you work with the model, you will soon find yourself customizing it to fit the particular business model that you have been planning or are looking for as an investment. For instance, put detail into the cells for projecting what if scenarios. Such analyses

can help increase your understanding of changes that the company may make to place themselves into a more favorable position in the market. You can then make certain assumptions about the company and this will help you in your decision process. Then Pattern Templates will become your own personal model of the economics of your investments and businesses that represent your portfolio.

Suggested Use of Sample Company Graphs

The samples provided on the CD provide templates that can be re-used. Compare the company you wish to analyze to the samples provided. Look for similarities in the data. If you can identify a sample that approximates the ranges of data for the new company you wish to work with, you will not have to modify the coordinates of the graphs. Just erase the sample data and fill in the new company's data.

If no such similarities can be found, then use the blanks, but be aware you may have to modify the graph coordinates to get a meaningful picture of the pattern.

Troubleshooting Tips

Windows:

If you experience any performance problems, please be aware of these basic system requirements that seem to be more of an issue with Window based operating systems than others.

- A 386 processor or better
- 4 megabytes of RAM or better
- Windows 3.1x at the very minimum
- Windows Permanent Swap File
- 256 Color display
- CD-ROM Drive (double speed recommended)

Bibliography

Ichak Adizes, *Corporate Lifecycles: How and Why Corporations Grow and Die and What to Do About It.* Prentice Hall Press; 1990.

Joseph Badaracco Jr., *Leading Quietly.* Harvard Business School Press; 2002.

Peter Block, *Stewardship: Choosing Service over Self Interest.* Berrett-Koehler; 1993.

John Bogle, *Bogle on Mutual Funds, New Perspectives for the Intelligent Investor.* McGraw-Hill Trade; 1993.

Mary Buffett, *Buffettology, The Previously Unexplained Techniques That Have Made Warren Buffett the World's Most Famous Investor.* Fireside; 1997

James C. Collins and Jerry I. Porras, *Built to Last: Successful Habits of Visionary Companies.* HarperCollins, 1994.

Arie De Geus, *The Living Company.* Harvard Business School Press; 1997.

Charles Ellis, *Winning the Loser's Game, Timeless Strategies for Successful Investing.* McGraw-Hill; 1998.

James Gleick, *Chaos: Making a New Science.* Penguin Books; 1987.

Eliyahu M. Goldratt & Jeff Cox, *The Goal, A Process of Ongoing Improvement.* North River Press; 1984.

Eliyahu M. Goldratt, *It's Not Luck*. North River Press; 1994. (This is Eliyahu Goldratt's sequel to *The Goal* focusing on the TOC Thinking processes.)

Benjamin Graham, *The Intelligent Investor: A Book of Practical Counsel*. Fourth Revised Edition; HarperCollins; 1973.

Joseph Jaworski, *Synchronicity: The Inner Path of Leadership*. Berrett-Koehler; 1996.

Robert Hagstrom, *The Warren Buffett Way, Investment Strategies of the World's Greatest Investor*. John Wiley & Sons, Inc.; 1995.

Robert Hagstrom, *The Warren Buffett Portfolio, Mastering the Power of the Focus Investment Strategy*. John Wiley & Sons, Inc.; 1999.

Thomas Johnson and Robert Kaplan, *Relevance Lost: The Rise and fall of Management Accounting*. Harvard Business School Press; 1987.

Peter Lynch, *One Up on Wall Street, How to Use What You Already Know to Make Money in the Market*. Fireside; 1989.

Peter Lynch, *Beating the Street* Fireside; 1993.

Geoffrey Moore, *Crossing the Chasm*. HarperCollins; 1995.

Geoffrey Moore, *Inside The Tornado: Marketing Strategies from Silicon Valley's Cutting Edge*.; HarperCollins; 1999.

Virginia Postrel, *The Future and Its Enemies: The Growing Conflict over Creativity, Enterprise and Progress*. Free Press; 1998.

Steven Sample, *The Contrarian's Guide to Leadership*. Jossey-Bass; 2002.

Adrian Slywotzky and David Morrison, *Profit Patterns. 30 ways to anticipate and profit from strategic forces reshaping your business*. Times Business Random House; 1999.

Michael Treacy and Fred Wiersema, *The Discipline of Market Leaders: Choose your Customers, Narrow your Focus, Dominate your Market. Perseus Publishing. 1997*

James Womack, Daniel Jones, and Daniel Roos, *The Machine that Changed the World, The Story of Lean Production. HarperCollins 1991.*

Web Based Resources:

annualreportservice.com
bloomberg.com
businessweek.com
edgarscan.pwc.global.com
finance.yahoo.com
freeedgar.com
investors.com
moneycentral.msn.com/investor/home.asp
money.cnn.com
moodys.com
morningstar.com
multexinvestor.com
prars.com
quicken.com
sec.gov
spoutlookonline.com
standardandpoors.com
starmine.com
thestreet.com
valueline.com

For more information about the authors of this book,
please visit:
www.aarongroupventures.com
www.cioam.com

For information on other publications by
North River Press, please visit:
www.northriverpress.com